An Ayah A Day

An Ayah A Day

365 Quranic Verses
To Uplift Your Spirit
and
Feed Your Soul

By Nadwa Zahid

FONS VITAE

First published in 2022 by
Fons Vitae
49 Mockingbird Valley Drive
Louisville, KY 40207
http://www.fonsvitae.com
Email: fonsvitaeky@aol.com

ISBN 978-1941610-886

Library of Congress Control Number: 2021949612

Cover design credit to Hazem Sannib

Printed in Canada

Verses 2:201, 2:277, 5:15, 6:102, 6:161 10:25, 14:1, 14:31, 17:9, 17:105, 22:64, 24:38, 24:42, 25:70, 31:3, 31:5, 31:8, 46:13, 55:12, 87:18, 88:15, 95:6 from The Study Quran by Seyyed Hossein Nasr, Caner K. Dagli, Maria Massi Dakake, Joseph E.B. Lumbard, Mohammed Rustom. Copyright © Seyyed Hossein Nasr. Used by permission of HarperCollins Publishers.

Verses 2:131, 2:155, 33:41, 44:55, and 95:5 used by permission of Kazi Publications.

أَلَا بِذِكْرِ اللَّهِ تَطْمَئِنُّ الْقُلُوبُ

In loving memory of my mother Ghada (1959-2005)

Contents

CONTENTS, CONTINUED

Background

I am a mother of two and have experienced extremely painful personal losses in my life. My mother passed away suddenly at the age of 45 in 2005. My grandfather whom I loved dearly died eight months later. I suffered multiple miscarriages and in 2006, when I was five and a half months pregnant, I lost my baby boy. Each was a sudden and unexpected loss and they just kept coming one after the other. In the midst of all this, I was also having to deal with all the trauma that came from a difficult marriage. All of these experiences led me down the path of seeking spiritual practices, which included holistic healing, meditation and mindfulness.

In 2015, as I was going through a long and difficult divorce with two young children to take care of, I was physically and emotionally drained. I no longer had the energy that I needed to get me through this next of life's hurdles. It was during the final stages of my divorce, that I sought comfort in the Holy Qur'an. I remember it was the month of Ramadan, and I was at a point when I was doing a lot of soul searching. My mother was my rock and her loss left me floundering. Not having her around, I felt lost and in need of guidance.

Desperately needing answers, I opened the Holy Book and began to read. As it was the month of Ramadan, I made the intention to read the Qur'an and to finish it by the end of the month. I had made that same intention many times in the past but was never able to complete it in time. This time Subhan Allah, perhaps my intention was pure and God knew of my desperation. I was able to read the Qur'an and finish it not once, but twice before the end of Ramadan. Not long into my daily recitation, I began to feel the words coming out of the page as though God were talking to me. I found myself weeping at some verses, smiling at others and sometimes even laughing from joy. I felt a complete sense of calm, peace and serenity with others. I reached out for my yellow highlighter and as I continued to read, I began to highlight the verses which I felt I had a deep connection with. The more I read the more I felt guided, supported and loved; Subhan Allah. All the answers I was looking for were right there in front of me. The selection of verses that made it into this volume are the ones that "talked" to me. These are the verses that helped me heal and find my way in life again. I have been graced with an inner-strength and peace from a new-found understanding and appreciation of my faith.

Not long after I finished reading the Qur'an, I decided to type out the verses which I had highlighted, and this is how the idea of this book was born. In a way I was seeking guidance and comfort for my own self and in doing so I found myself wanting to share that same experience with the world.

An Ayah A Day is a spiritual compendium and guide. The way I have laid out the book is by writing one verse in Arabic with the English translation underneath on each page, hoping it can be read and serve as a day book. There is plenty of empty space beneath each verse, intended for the reader's personal reflections. Use that space to journal your own experience, reflect on how that particular verse made you feel or even write down how you could put that verse into action. *An Ayah A Day* is more than just a collection of verses, it is a daily opportunity for you to consider and apply these counsels to your daily life. Take time to just sit with the verse for a few minutes and truly contemplate its meaning, its message and how it resonates with you on a truly personal level. This is your special time to converse with Allah. Allow Him to speak to you through His words.

Although the verses are from the Holy Qur'an my hope is that this small journal will resonate not only with Muslims, but with non-Muslims as well. I pray these verses will touch hearts far and wide, at a time when many of us have lost the way, lost hope and are in despair. For many years my manuscript sat untouched on my laptop, waiting for the right time to see it to fruition. It was during lockdown in 2020, that I was suddenly inspired to complete the work and finally get this volume published. Between Covid and the effect it has had on our overall health, wealth, and mental well-being, as well as the geopolitical unrest that we see unfolding all around us, I realised that people needed this now more than ever. We need to raise our vibration of hope, of faith, of love and of community.

There is a prayer which I have been saying in the last *sajdah* of each prayer ever since my mother passed away and that is (*Al-Ahqaf* 46:15). The translation is in the book.

"رَبِّ أَوْزِعْنِي أَنْ أَشْكُرَ نِعْمَتَكَ الَّتِي أَنْعَمْتَ عَلَيَّ وَعَلَىٰ والِدَيَّ وَأَنْ أَعْمَلَ صالِحًا تَرْضاهُ وَأَصْلِحْ لِي فِي ذُرِّيَّتِي ۖ إِنِّي تُبْتُ إِلَيْكَ وَإِنِّي مِنَ المُسْلِمِينَ"

This is my *sadaqa jariya*, my contribution and my gift; to my parents, to my children and to past and future generations.

May God Almighty Guide, Protect and Bless Us All.

Ameen

بَلِّغُوا عَنِّي وَلَوْ آيَةً

"Convey from me, even if it is one verse"
Prophet Muhammad (Sahih Al-Bukhari)

Introduction

For many years, I have admired the great poetry of Rumi and Khalil Gibran and recently found myself wondering why there was not something similar based on the words of Allah ﷻ. After all, there is no greater supremacy than Allah ﷻ and no words wiser, greater or more absolute than His.

The idea for this book came about in 2015 when I was reciting the Qur'an during the holy month of Ramadan. While reading the Qur'an from cover-to-cover; certain verses began to resonate with me on a very deep level. I found myself feeling completely at peace, comforted, loved and protected by the absolute beauty, perfection and flawlessness of Allah's words: *"God is the Light of the heavens and the earth."* In Allah's words I found great healing and guidance. As Imam Ali once said, "The words of Allah are the medicine of the heart", and this was definitely true for me. Writer A. Helwa put it beautifully when she said, "On the darkest nights of our souls, the Qur'an is a faithful companion with embracing arms. For every feeling we are experiencing, the Qur'an has a soothing verse, and for every pain we carry, it has a timeless remedy."

I believe we Muslims have become so focused on the *Shari'a* that we have moved away from the true essence of Islam – from the 'heart' of Islam – its spirituality. It is only through spirituality that we can learn how to truly love. *"It is not the eyes that go blind, but the hearts within the breasts that go blind."* By following the spiritual path, we learn how to open our hearts and how to keep our hearts open – not just during times of happiness, but in times of hardship as well.

Hasan Gai Eaton wrote, "Islam teaches resignation, which is a state of happiness that rises above the blows of fate." I firmly believe this to be true; only by deepening our spirituality do we become enlightened and find inner-peace. It is in this state of enlightenment that our perspective begins to shift and we are able to see the world with joy, filled with beauty. *"God is beautiful, He loves beauty."* If we approach everything that we do in life with love – learn with love, teach with love and communicate with love – if we allow love to guide us and lead the way so that we may become more heart-centred – then we will be able to forgive through love, let go of anger, fear and grief through love. Overcome loss, insecurity, aggression and sadness through love. If we did that, and applied love every step of the way, then our entire experience on this earth would be very different. *"Do you not see that everything in the heavens and everything that is on the earth pays adoration to God: the sun and the moon and the stars, the mountains and the trees and the beasts and many among mankind?"*

By being heart-centred we will forgive rather than react, becoming more gentle, humble and compassionate; *"Wherever you turn, there is the Face of God."* The inner-peace which most of us so desperately seek will no longer be a wishful thought or an abstract illusion, but can become something attainable for us all.

This book is not intended for Muslims alone. Indeed, it is meant for anyone searching for comfort and peace. In the words of our beloved Prophet Muhammad ﷺ *"Let the Qur'an be the springtime of my heart, the light of my chest, the remover of my sadness, and the pacifier of my worries."*

The verses selected are meant to help the reader stop, think, contemplate, wonder and marvel at the meaning and beauty of this life and the hereafter; *"Their skins and their hearts soften at the remembrance of God."*

We are living in a time when the image of Islam has been damaged and tarnished by both Muslims and non-Muslims. I hope this collection of verses sheds some light on the true essence of Islam. The Islam that I know and love. The Islam of hope, kindness and mercy; of tolerance, forgiveness, patience and most of all, of peace, love and compassion; *"Peace!" A word from a Lord most Merciful."*

The translations of the Qur'an used as references are from various scholars and translators including Mohammad Asad, M.A.S Abdel Haleem, Muhammad Pickthall and Dr. Hossein Nasr.

I hope these verses touch your heart, mind and soul as they did mine, for *"Truly it is in the remembrance of God that hearts find peace."*

رَب زِدني عِلماً

Your sister,
Nadwa Zahid

بِسْمِ اللَّهِ الرَّحْمٰنِ الرَّحِيمِ

اقْرَأْ بِاسْمِ رَبِّكَ الَّذِي خَلَقَ ﴿١﴾ خَلَقَ الْإِنْسَانَ مِنْ عَلَقٍ ﴿٢﴾ اقْرَأْ وَرَبُّكَ الْأَكْرَمُ ﴿٣﴾ الَّذِي عَلَّمَ بِالْقَلَمِ ﴿٤﴾ عَلَّمَ الْإِنْسَانَ مَا لَمْ يَعْلَمْ ﴿٥﴾

Read! In the name of thy Lord who created (1) Created man from a blood clot (2) Read! Thy Lord is most Bountiful (3) Who taught by the Pen (4) Taught man what he knows not (5)

بِسْمِ اللَّهِ الرَّحْمَٰنِ الرَّحِيمِ

الْحَمْدُ لِلَّهِ رَبِّ الْعَالَمِينَ ﴿٢﴾ الرَّحْمَٰنِ الرَّحِيمِ ﴿٣﴾ مَالِكِ يَوْمِ الدِّينِ ﴿٤﴾ إِيَّاكَ نَعْبُدُ وَإِيَّاكَ نَسْتَعِينُ ﴿٥﴾ اهْدِنَا الصِّرَاطَ الْمُسْتَقِيمَ ﴿٦﴾ صِرَاطَ الَّذِينَ أَنْعَمْتَ عَلَيْهِمْ غَيْرِ الْمَغْضُوبِ عَلَيْهِمْ وَلَا الضَّالِّينَ ﴿٧﴾ ﴿الفاتحة﴾

In the name of God, the Compassionate the Merciful (1) Praise be to God, Lord of the Worlds (2) The Compassionate the Merciful (3) Master of the Day of Judgement (4) Thee alone we worship and Thee alone we ask for help (5) Guide us upon the straight path (6) The path of those whom You have blessed; not (the path) of those who earn Your wrath nor of those who have gone astray (7)

Al-Fatiha (The Opening) 1:1-7

الم ﴿١﴾ ذَلِكَ الْكِتَابُ لَا رَيْبَ ۛ فِيهِ ۛ هُدًى لِلْمُتَّقِينَ ﴿٢﴾ الَّذِينَ يُؤْمِنُونَ بِالْغَيْبِ وَيُقِيمُونَ الصَّلَاةَ وَمِمَّا رَزَقْنَاهُمْ يُنْفِقُونَ ﴿٣﴾ وَالَّذِينَ يُؤْمِنُونَ بِمَا أُنْزِلَ إِلَيْكَ وَمَا أُنْزِلَ مِنْ قَبْلِكَ وَبِالْآخِرَةِ هُمْ يُوقِنُونَ ﴿٤﴾ أُولَئِكَ عَلَى هُدًى مِنْ رَبِّهِمْ ۖ وَأُولَئِكَ هُمُ الْمُفْلِحُونَ ﴿٥﴾ ﴿البقرة﴾

Alif. Lām. Mīm (1) This is the Scripture; in which there is no doubt, guidance for all those who are mindful of God (2) Who believe in the Unseen, are steadfast in prayer and spend of what We have bestowed upon them (3) And who believe in what was sent down unto you (Muhammad) and in what was sent down before you, and who are certain of the Hereafter (4) It is they who are on (true) guidance from their Lord and it is they who shall prosper (5)

Al-Baqarah (The Cow) 2:1-5

يَا أَيُّهَا النَّاسُ اعْبُدُوا رَبَّكُمُ الَّذِي خَلَقَكُمْ وَالَّذِينَ مِنْ قَبْلِكُمْ لَعَلَّكُمْ تَتَّقُونَ ﴿٢١﴾ الَّذِي جَعَلَ لَكُمُ الْأَرْضَ فِرَاشًا وَالسَّمَاءَ بِنَاءً وَأَنْزَلَ مِنَ السَّمَاءِ مَاءً فَأَخْرَجَ بِهِ مِنَ الثَّمَرَاتِ رِزْقًا لَكُمْ فَلَا تَجْعَلُوا لِلَّهِ أَنْدَادًا وَأَنْتُمْ تَعْلَمُونَ ﴿٢٢﴾ ﴿البقرة﴾

O mankind! Worship your Lord who created you and those who were before you, so that you may be mindful (of God) (21) Who made the earth a resting place for you and the sky a canopy, and sent down water from the sky and thereby brought forth fruits for your sustenance; do not then knowing this set up rivals to God (22)

Al-Baqarah (The Cow) 2:21-22

وَبَشِّرِ الَّذِينَ آمَنُوا وَعَمِلُوا الصَّالِحَاتِ أَنَّ لَهُمْ جَنَّاتٍ تَجْرِي مِنْ تَحْتِهَا الْأَنْهَارُ ۖ كُلَّمَا رُزِقُوا مِنْهَا مِنْ ثَمَرَةٍ رِزْقًا ۙ قَالُوا هَٰذَا الَّذِي رُزِقْنَا مِنْ قَبْلُ ۖ وَأُتُوا بِهِ مُتَشَابِهًا ۖ وَلَهُمْ فِيهَا أَزْوَاجٌ مُطَهَّرَةٌ ۖ وَهُمْ فِيهَا خَالِدُونَ ﴿٢٥﴾ ﴿البقرة﴾

And give glad tidings to those who believe and perform righteous deeds that theirs shall be Gardens beneath which rivers flow; whenever they are provided with fruits as provision, they shall say, "This is the provision we were given before", and they shall be given it in resemblance, and there shall be for them spouses purified, and therein they shall abide (25)

Al-Baqarah (The Cow) 2:25

قُلْنَا اهْبِطُوا مِنْهَا جَمِيعًا ۖ فَإِمَّا يَأْتِيَنَّكُم مِّنِّي هُدًى فَمَن تَبِعَ هُدَايَ فَلَا خَوْفٌ عَلَيْهِمْ وَلَا هُمْ يَحْزَنُونَ ﴿٣٨﴾ ﴿البقرة﴾

We said "Get down from it, all of you. There shall most certainly come unto you guidance from Me, and those who follow My guidance no fear shall come upon them nor shall they grieve" (38)

Al-Baqarah (The Cow) 2:38

وَآمِنُوا بِمَا أَنْزَلْتُ مُصَدِّقًا لِمَا مَعَكُمْ وَلَا تَكُونُوا أَوَّلَ كَافِرٍ بِهِ ۖ وَلَا تَشْتَرُوا

بِآيَاتِي ثَمَنًا قَلِيلًا وَإِيَّايَ فَاتَّقُونِ ﴿٤١﴾ ﴿البقرة﴾

And believe in that which I have sent down, confirming that which you already possess, and do not be the first to disbelieve in it. And do not sell My revelations for a trifling price and be mindful of Me (41)

Al-Baqarah (The Cow) 2:41

وَلَا تَلْبِسُوا الْحَقَّ بِالْبَاطِلِ وَتَكْتُمُوا الْحَقَّ وَأَنْتُمْ تَعْلَمُونَ ﴿٤٢﴾ ﴿البقرة﴾

And do not cover the truth with falsehood, nor knowingly conceal the truth (42)

Al-Baqarah (The Cow) 2:42

وَأَقِيمُوا الصَّلَاةَ وَآتُوا الزَّكَاةَ وَارْكَعُوا مَعَ الرَّاكِعِينَ ﴿٤٣﴾ ﴿البقرة﴾

And be steadfast in prayer, and pay the alms, and bow down with those who bow (in worship) (43)

Al-Baqarah (The Cow) 2:43

وَاسْتَعِينُوا بِالصَّبْرِ وَالصَّلَاةِ ۚ وَإِنَّهَا لَكَبِيرَةٌ إِلَّا عَلَى الْخَاشِعِينَ ﴿٤٥﴾ الَّذِينَ يَظُنُّونَ أَنَّهُم مُّلَاقُو رَبِّهِمْ وَأَنَّهُمْ إِلَيْهِ رَاجِعُونَ ﴿٤٦﴾ ﴿البقرة﴾

And seek help in patience and prayer; for it is indeed difficult except for the humble (45) Who know that they will meet their Lord and that unto Him they shall return (46)

Al-Baqarah (The Cow) 2:45-46

إِنَّ الَّذِينَ آمَنُوا وَالَّذِينَ هَادُوا وَالنَّصَارَىٰ وَالصَّابِئِينَ مَنْ آمَنَ بِاللَّهِ وَالْيَوْمِ

الْآخِرِ وَعَمِلَ صَالِحًا فَلَهُمْ أَجْرُهُمْ عِنْدَ رَبِّهِمْ وَلَا خَوْفٌ عَلَيْهِمْ وَلَا هُمْ

يَحْزَنُونَ ﴿٦٢﴾ ﴿البقرة﴾

Truly, those who believe (in that which is revealed unto thee, Muhammad), and the Jews, and the Christians, and Sabians – whoever believes in God and the Last Day and performs righteous deeds shall have their reward with their Lord and no fear shall come upon them nor shall they grieve (62)

Al-Baqarah (The Cow) 2:62

أَلَمْ تَعْلَمْ أَنَّ اللَّهَ لَهُ مُلْكُ السَّمَاوَاتِ وَالْأَرْضِ ۚ وَمَا لَكُمْ مِنْ دُونِ اللَّهِ مِنْ

وَلِيٍّ وَلَا نَصِيرٍ ﴿١٠٧﴾ ﴿البقرة﴾

Do you not know that God is Sovereign over the heavens and the earth, and that besides God you have neither protector nor helper? (107)

Al-Baqarah (The Cow) 2:107

وَأَقِيمُوا الصَّلَاةَ وَآتُوا الزَّكَاةَ ۚ وَمَا تُقَدِّمُوا لِأَنْفُسِكُمْ مِنْ خَيْرٍ تَجِدُوهُ عِنْدَ اللَّهِ ۚ إِنَّ اللَّهَ بِمَا تَعْمَلُونَ بَصِيرٌ ﴿١١٠﴾ ﴿البقرة﴾

And be steadfast in prayer and give the alms, and whatever you send forth for your souls of good (deeds), you will find it with God. Truly God sees all that you do (110)

Al-Baqarah (The Cow) 2:110

بَلَىٰ مَنْ أَسْلَمَ وَجْهَهُ لِلَّهِ وَهُوَ مُحْسِنٌ فَلَهُ أَجْرُهُ عِنْدَ رَبِّهِ وَلَا خَوْفٌ عَلَيْهِمْ
وَلَا هُمْ يَحْزَنُونَ ﴿١١٢﴾ ﴿البقرة﴾

Truly! Whoever submits himself completely to God and is virtuous, shall have their reward with their Lord and no fear shall come upon them, nor shall they grieve (112)

Al-Baqarah (The Cow) 2:112

وَلِلَّهِ المَشرِقُ وَالمَغرِبُ ، فَأَينَما تُوَلّوا فَثَمَّ وَجهُ اللَّهِ ، إِنَّ اللَّهَ واسِعٌ عَليمٌ

﴿١١٥﴾ ﴿البقرة﴾

To God belongs the East and the West, and wherever you turn there is God's Face. Truly God is Infinite, Knowing (115)

Al-Baqarah (The Cow) 2:115

بَدِيعُ السَّمَاوَاتِ وَالْأَرْضِ ۖ وَإِذَا قَضَىٰ أَمْرًا فَإِنَّمَا يَقُولُ لَهُ كُنْ فَيَكُونُ ﴿١١٧﴾

﴿البقرة﴾

The Originator of the heavens and the earth, and when He decrees a thing, He only says unto it "Be!" and it is (117)

Al-Baqarah (The Cow) 2:117

وَاتَّقُوا يَوْمًا لَا تَجْزِي نَفْسٌ عَنْ نَفْسٍ شَيْئًا وَلَا يُقْبَلُ مِنْهَا عَدْلٌ وَلَا تَنْفَعُهَا شَفَاعَةٌ وَلَا هُمْ يُنْصَرُونَ ﴿١٢٣﴾ ﴿البقرة﴾

And be mindful of a Day when no soul shall avail another, nor shall compensation be accepted from it, nor shall intercession be of use to it, nor will they be helped (123)

Al-Baqarah (The Cow) 2:123

وَإِذْ يَرْفَعُ إِبْرَاهِيمُ الْقَوَاعِدَ مِنَ الْبَيْتِ وَإِسْمَاعِيلُ رَبَّنَا تَقَبَّلْ مِنَّا۔إِنَّكَ أَنْتَ السَّمِيعُ الْعَلِيمُ ﴿١٢٧﴾ رَبَّنَا وَاجْعَلْنَا مُسْلِمَيْنِ لَكَ وَمِنْ ذُرِّيَّتِنَا أُمَّةً مُسْلِمَةً لَكَ وَأَرِنَا مَنَاسِكَنَا وَتُبْ عَلَيْنَا۔ إِنَّكَ أَنْتَ التَّوَّابُ الرَّحِيمُ ﴿١٢٨﴾ رَبَّنَا وَابْعَثْ فِيهِمْ رَسُولًا مِنْهُمْ يَتْلُو عَلَيْهِمْ آيَاتِكَ وَيُعَلِّمُهُمُ الْكِتَابَ وَالْحِكْمَةَ وَيُزَكِّيهِمْ ۚ إِنَّكَ أَنْتَ الْعَزِيزُ الْحَكِيمُ ﴿١٢٩﴾ ﴿البقرة﴾

And when Abraham and Ishmael were raising the foundations of the House, (they prayed) "Our Lord, accept this from us, for truly Thou (alone) art the Hearing, the Knowing (127) Our Lord, and make us submit (our will) unto Thee and of our descendants a community submissive unto Thee, and show us our ways of worship, and accept our repentance. Truly, Thou art the Relenting, the Merciful (128) Our Lord and raise up in their midst a messenger from among them who will recite unto them Thy revelations, and will teach them the Scripture and Wisdom, and purify them. Truly Thou art the Almighty, the Wise" (129)

Al-Baqarah (The Cow) 2:127-129

إِذْ قَالَ لَهُ رَبُّهُ أَسْلِمْ ـ قَالَ أَسْلَمْتُ لِرَبِّ الْعَالَمِينَ ﴿١٣١﴾ ﴿البقرة﴾

When his Lord said to him Surrender! He said, "I have surrendered to the Lord of the Worlds" (131)

Al-Baqarah (The Cow) 2:131

وَكَذَلِكَ جَعَلْنَاكُمْ أُمَّةً وَسَطًا لِتَكُونُوا شُهَدَاءَ عَلَى النَّاسِ وَيَكُونَ الرَّسُولُ عَلَيْكُمْ شَهِيدًا ۗ وَمَا جَعَلْنَا الْقِبْلَةَ الَّتِي كُنْتَ عَلَيْهَا إِلَّا لِنَعْلَمَ مَنْ يَتَّبِعُ الرَّسُولَ مِمَّنْ يَنْقَلِبُ عَلَىٰ عَقِبَيْهِ ۚ وَإِنْ كَانَتْ لَكَبِيرَةً إِلَّا عَلَى الَّذِينَ هَدَى اللَّهُ ۗ وَمَا كَانَ اللَّهُ لِيُضِيعَ إِيمَانَكُمْ ۚ إِنَّ اللَّهَ بِالنَّاسِ لَرَءُوفٌ رَحِيمٌ ﴿١٤٣﴾ ﴿البقرة﴾

Thus, We have made you a middle (just) nation so that you may bear witnesses for mankind, and that the Messenger may be a witness over you. And We only appointed the *qibla* which you had been following to know those who follow the Messenger from those who turn back on their heels and it was indeed difficult save for those whom God guided. But it was not God's purpose that your faith should be in vain, truly God is most Compassionate and Merciful towards mankind (143)

Al-Baqarah (The Cow) 2:143

وَلِكُلٍّ وِجْهَةٌ هُوَ مُوَلِّيهَا ۖ فَاسْتَبِقُوا الْخَيْرَاتِ ۚ أَيْنَ مَا تَكُونُوا يَأْتِ بِكُمُ اللَّهُ جَمِيعًا ۚ إِنَّ اللَّهَ عَلَىٰ كُلِّ شَيْءٍ قَدِيرٌ ﴿١٤٨﴾ ﴿البقرة﴾

Everyone has a direction toward which he turns. So strive with one another in doing good and wherever you are God will bring you together. Truly God is Powerful over all things (148)

Al-Baqarah (The Cow) 2:148

فَاذْكُرُونِي أَذْكُرْكُمْ وَاشْكُرُوا لِي وَلَا تَكْفُرُونِ ﴿١٥٢﴾ ﴿البقرة﴾

So remember Me, I will remember you. And give thanks to Me and disbelieve in Me not (152)

Al-Baqarah (The Cow) 2:152

يَا أَيُّهَا الَّذِينَ آمَنُوا اسْتَعِينُوا بِالصَّبْرِ وَالصَّلَاةِ ۚ إِنَّ اللَّهَ مَعَ الصَّابِرِينَ ﴿١٥٣﴾ ﴿البقرة﴾

O you who believe! Seek help through patience and prayer, truly God is with the patient (153)

Al-Baqarah (The Cow) 2:153

وَلَا تَقُولُوا لِمَنْ يُقْتَلُ فِي سَبِيلِ اللَّهِ أَمْوَاتٌ ۚ بَلْ أَحْيَاءٌ وَلَٰكِنْ لَا تَشْعُرُونَ ﴿١٥٤﴾ ﴿البقرة﴾

And say not of those who are slain in God's cause "They are dead". Nay, they are alive, but you are unaware (154)

Al-Baqarah (The Cow) 2:154

وَلَنَبْلُوَنَّكُم بِشَيْءٍ مِنَ الْخَوْفِ وَالْجُوعِ وَنَقْصٍ مِنَ الْأَمْوَالِ وَالْأَنْفُسِ وَالثَّمَرَاتِ ۗ وَبَشِّرِ الصَّابِرِينَ ﴿١٥٥﴾ ﴿البقرة﴾

And We shall certainly test you with something of fear and hunger, and loss of wealth and lives and crops; but give glad tidings to the steadfast (155)

Al-Baqarah (The Cow) 2:155

الَّذِينَ إِذَا أَصَابَتْهُمْ مُصِيبَةٌ قَالُوا إِنَّا لِلَّهِ وَإِنَّا إِلَيْهِ رَاجِعُونَ ﴿١٥٦﴾ أُولَٰئِكَ عَلَيْهِمْ صَلَوَاتٌ مِنْ رَبِّهِمْ وَرَحْمَةٌ ۖ وَأُولَٰئِكَ هُمُ الْمُهْتَدُونَ ﴿١٥٧﴾ ﴿البقرة﴾

Those who when calamity befalls them, say "Truly we belong to God and unto Him we shall return" (156) It is they upon whom come blessings from their Lord and mercy, they are the rightly guided (157)

Al-Baqarah (The Cow) 2:156-157

وَإِلَٰهُكُمْ إِلَٰهٌ وَاحِدٌ ۖ لَا إِلَٰهَ إِلَّا هُوَ الرَّحْمَٰنُ الرَّحِيمُ ﴿١٦٣﴾ ﴿البقرة﴾

And your God is one God, there is no god but Him, the Compassionate, the Merciful (163)

Al-Baqarah (The Cow) 2:163

إِنَّ فِي خَلْقِ السَّمَاوَاتِ وَالْأَرْضِ وَاخْتِلَافِ اللَّيْلِ وَالنَّهَارِ وَالْفُلْكِ الَّتِي تَجْرِي فِي الْبَحْرِ بِمَا يَنْفَعُ النَّاسَ وَمَا أَنْزَلَ اللَّهُ مِنَ السَّمَاءِ مِنْ مَاءٍ فَأَحْيَا بِهِ الْأَرْضَ بَعْدَ مَوْتِهَا وَبَثَّ فِيهَا مِنْ كُلِّ دَابَّةٍ وَتَصْرِيفِ الرِّيَاحِ وَالسَّحَابِ الْمُسَخَّرِ بَيْنَ السَّمَاءِ وَالْأَرْضِ لَآيَاتٍ لِقَوْمٍ يَعْقِلُونَ ﴿١٦٤﴾ ﴿البقرة﴾

Indeed in the creation of the heavens and the earth, and the succession of night and day; and in the ships that run upon the sea with what is useful to man; and in the water which God sends down from the sky, thereby reviving the earth after its death, scattering all manner of living creatures thereon; and in the change of the winds and the clouds that run their appointed course between the sky and the earth are surely signs for a people who use their intellect (164)

Al-Baqarah (The Cow) 2:164

لَيْسَ الْبِرَّ أَنْ تُوَلُّوا وُجُوهَكُمْ قِبَلَ الْمَشْرِقِ وَالْمَغْرِبِ وَلَٰكِنَّ الْبِرَّ مَنْ آمَنَ بِاللَّهِ وَالْيَوْمِ الْآخِرِ وَالْمَلَائِكَةِ وَالْكِتَابِ وَالنَّبِيِّينَ وَآتَى الْمَالَ عَلَىٰ حُبِّهِ ذَوِي الْقُرْبَىٰ وَالْيَتَامَىٰ وَالْمَسَاكِينَ وَابْنَ السَّبِيلِ وَالسَّائِلِينَ وَفِي الرِّقَابِ وَأَقَامَ الصَّلَاةَ وَآتَى الزَّكَاةَ وَالْمُوفُونَ بِعَهْدِهِمْ إِذَا عَاهَدُوا ۖ وَالصَّابِرِينَ فِي الْبَأْسَاءِ وَالضَّرَّاءِ وَحِينَ الْبَأْسِ ۗ أُولَٰئِكَ الَّذِينَ صَدَقُوا ۖ وَأُولَٰئِكَ هُمُ الْمُتَّقُونَ ﴿١٧٧﴾ البقرة

Piety is not that you turn your faces to the East or to the West. Rather, piety is he who believes in God and the Last Day and the angels and the Scripture and the prophets; and gives of his substance, however cherished, to kinsfolk, and the orphans, and the needy, and the wayfarer, and the beggars and to set slaves free; and is constant in prayer and gives the alms; and those who fulfil their oaths when they pledge them, and the patient in misfortune and adversity and in times of peril. It is they who are the sincere, and it is they who are the God-conscious (177)

Al-Baqarah (The Cow) 2:177

يَا أَيُّهَا الَّذِينَ آمَنُوا كُتِبَ عَلَيْكُمُ الْقِصَاصُ فِي الْقَتْلَى ـ الْحُرُّ بِالْحُرِّ وَالْعَبْدُ بِالْعَبْدِ وَالْأُنْثَىٰ بِالْأُنْثَىٰ ۚ فَمَنْ عُفِيَ لَهُ مِنْ أَخِيهِ شَيْءٌ فَاتِّبَاعٌ بِالْمَعْرُوفِ وَأَدَاءٌ إِلَيْهِ بِإِحْسَانٍ ۗ ذَٰلِكَ تَخْفِيفٌ مِنْ رَبِّكُمْ وَرَحْمَةٌ ۗ فَمَنِ اعْتَدَىٰ بَعْدَ ذَٰلِكَ فَلَهُ عَذَابٌ أَلِيمٌ ﴿١٧٨﴾ ﴿البقرة﴾

O you who believe! Just retribution is ordained for you in the matter of the slain; the free for the free, and the slave for the slave, and the female for the female. But for one who receives any pardon from his brother, let it be adhered to fairly, and restitution made to him with goodness. That is an alleviation from your Lord and a mercy. Whoever transgresses after that shall have an agonizing torment (178)

Al-Baqarah (The Cow) 2:178

يا أَيُّهَا الَّذِينَ آمَنوا كُتِبَ عَلَيكُمُ الصِّيامُ كَما كُتِبَ عَلَى الَّذِينَ مِن قَبلِكُم لَعَلَّكُم تَتَّقونَ ﴿١٨٣﴾ ﴿البقرة﴾

O you who believe! Fasting is ordained for you as it was ordained to those before you, so that you may be mindful (of God) (183)

Al-Baqarah (The Cow) 2:183

وَإِذَا سَأَلَكَ عِبَادِي عَنِّي فَإِنِّي قَرِيبٌ ـ أُجِيبُ دَعْوَةَ الدَّاعِ إِذَا دَعَانِ ـ

فَلْيَسْتَجِيبُوا لِي وَلْيُؤْمِنُوا بِي لَعَلَّهُمْ يَرْشُدُونَ ﴿١٨٦﴾ ﴿البقرة﴾

And if My servants ask you about Me, truly I am near. I respond to the call of the caller whenever he calls Me. So let them respond to Me and believe in Me, so that they may be guided (186)

Al-Baqarah (The Cow) 2:186

أُحِلَّ لَكُمْ لَيْلَةَ الصِّيَامِ الرَّفَثُ إِلَىٰ نِسَائِكُمْ ۚ هُنَّ لِبَاسٌ لَكُمْ وَأَنْتُمْ لِبَاسٌ لَهُنَّ ۗ عَلِمَ اللَّهُ أَنَّكُمْ كُنْتُمْ تَخْتَانُونَ أَنْفُسَكُمْ فَتَابَ عَلَيْكُمْ وَعَفَا عَنْكُمْ ۖ فَالْآنَ بَاشِرُوهُنَّ وَابْتَغُوا مَا كَتَبَ اللَّهُ لَكُمْ ۚ وَكُلُوا وَاشْرَبُوا حَتَّىٰ يَتَبَيَّنَ لَكُمُ الْخَيْطُ الْأَبْيَضُ مِنَ الْخَيْطِ الْأَسْوَدِ مِنَ الْفَجْرِ ۖ ثُمَّ أَتِمُّوا الصِّيَامَ إِلَى اللَّيْلِ ۚ وَلَا تُبَاشِرُوهُنَّ وَأَنْتُمْ عَاكِفُونَ فِي الْمَسَاجِدِ ۗ تِلْكَ حُدُودُ اللَّهِ فَلَا تَقْرَبُوهَا ۗ كَذَٰلِكَ يُبَيِّنُ اللَّهُ آيَاتِهِ لِلنَّاسِ لَعَلَّهُمْ يَتَّقُونَ ﴿١٨٧﴾ ﴿البقرة﴾

You have been permitted, on the nights of the fast, to go unto your wives. They are garments for you, and you are garments for them. God was aware that you were deceiving yourselves, so He turned unto you and pardoned you. So now lie with them and seek what God has prescribed for you, and eat and drink until the white thread becomes distinct from the black thread of the dawn. Then observe the fast until nightfall and do not lie with them while you are in devotional retreat in the mosques. These are the boundaries set by God so do not approach them. Thus does God make clear His signs to mankind, so that they might become conscious of Him (187)

Al-Baqarah (The Cow) 2:187

وَقَاتِلُوا فِي سَبِيلِ اللَّهِ الَّذِينَ يُقَاتِلُونَكُمْ وَلَا تَعْتَدُوا ۚ إِنَّ اللَّهَ لَا يُحِبُّ الْمُعْتَدِينَ ﴿١٩٠﴾ ﴿البقرة﴾

And fight in God's cause against those who wage war against you, but do not commit aggression — for truly, God does not love aggressors (190)

Al-Baqarah (The Cow) 2:190

الشَّهْرُ الْحَرَامُ بِالشَّهْرِ الْحَرَامِ وَالْحُرُمَاتُ قِصَاصٌ ۚ فَمَنِ اعْتَدَىٰ عَلَيْكُمْ

فَاعْتَدُوا عَلَيْهِ بِمِثْلِ مَا اعْتَدَىٰ عَلَيْكُمْ ۚ وَاتَّقُوا اللَّهَ وَاعْلَمُوا أَنَّ اللَّهَ مَعَ

الْمُتَّقِينَ ﴿١٩٤﴾ ﴿البقرة﴾

The sacred month for the sacred month, and violation of sanctity is just retribution. So whoever commits aggression against you, then commit aggression against him in like manner, and be mindful of God and know that God is with those who are mindful (of Him) (194)

Al-Baqarah (The Cow) 2:194

وَأَنْفِقُوا فِي سَبِيلِ اللَّهِ وَلَا تُلْقُوا بِأَيْدِيكُمْ إِلَى التَّهْلُكَةِ ۰ وَأَحْسِنُوا ۰ إِنَّ اللَّهَ يُحِبُّ الْمُحْسِنِينَ ﴿١٩٥﴾ ﴿البقرة﴾

And spend in God's cause; and do not cast yourselves by your own hands into destruction. And be virtuous, truly God loves the virtuous (195)

Al-Baqarah (The Cow) 2:195

وَمِنْهُم مَّن يَقُولُ رَبَّنَا آتِنَا فِي الدُّنْيَا حَسَنَةً وَفِي الْآخِرَةِ حَسَنَةً وَقِنَا عَذَابَ النَّارِ ﴿٢٠١﴾ أُولَٰئِكَ لَهُمْ نَصِيبٌ مِّمَّا كَسَبُوا ۚ وَاللَّهُ سَرِيعُ الْحِسَابِ ﴿٢٠٢﴾ ﴿البقرة﴾

And among them are those who say "Our Lord, give us good in this world and good in the Hereafter, and shield us from the punishment of the Fire!" (201) It is they who shall have a share of what they have earned, and God is swift in reckoning (202)

Al-Baqarah (The Cow) 2:201-202

وَمِنَ النَّاسِ مَنْ يَشْرِي نَفْسَهُ ابْتِغَاءَ مَرْضَاتِ اللَّهِ ۚ وَاللَّهُ رَءُوفٌ بِالْعِبَادِ

﴿٢٠٧﴾ ﴿البقرة﴾

And among mankind is one who sells his soul seeking God's pleasure,
and God is Compassionate with His servants (207)

Al-Baqarah (The Cow) 2:207

يَا أَيُّهَا الَّذِينَ آمَنُوا ادْخُلُوا فِي السِّلْمِ كَافَّةً وَلَا تَتَّبِعُوا خُطُوَاتِ الشَّيْطَانِ ۚ إِنَّهُ لَكُمْ عَدُوٌّ مُبِينٌ ﴿٢٠٨﴾ ﴿البقرة﴾

O you who believe! Enter wholeheartedly into submission unto God; and do not follow the footsteps of Satan, for to you he is a clear enemy (208)

Al-Baqarah (The Cow) 2:208

يَسْأَلُونَكَ مَاذَا يُنْفِقُونَ قُلْ مَا أَنْفَقْتُمْ مِنْ خَيْرٍ فَلِلْوَالِدَيْنِ وَالْأَقْرَبِينَ وَالْيَتَامَىٰ وَالْمَسَاكِينِ وَابْنِ السَّبِيلِ وَمَا تَفْعَلُوا مِنْ خَيْرٍ فَإِنَّ اللَّهَ بِهِ عَلِيمٌ ﴿٢١٥﴾ ﴿البقرة﴾

They ask thee (Muhammad) what they should spend. Say, "Whatever of your wealth you spend, let it be for your parents, and the kinsfolk and the orphans and the needy and the wayfarer. And whatever good you do, truly God knows it" (215)

Al-Baqarah (The Cow) 2:215

مَنْ ذَا الَّذِي يُقْرِضُ اللَّهَ قَرْضًا حَسَنًا فَيُضَاعِفَهُ لَهُ أَضْعَافًا كَثِيرَةً ۚ وَاللَّهُ يَقْبِضُ وَيَبْسُطُ وَإِلَيْهِ تُرْجَعُونَ ﴿٢٤٥﴾ ﴿البقرة﴾

Who shall lend unto God a goodly loan, which He will multiply for him many times over? God withholds and gives abundantly, and unto Him you shall return (245)

Al-Baqarah (The Cow) 2:245

اللَّهُ لَا إِلَهَ إِلَّا هُوَ الْحَيُّ الْقَيُّومُ ۚ لَا تَأْخُذُهُ سِنَةٌ وَلَا نَوْمٌ ۚ لَهُ مَا فِي السَّمَاوَاتِ وَمَا فِي الْأَرْضِ ۚ مَنْ ذَا الَّذِي يَشْفَعُ عِنْدَهُ إِلَّا بِإِذْنِهِ ۚ يَعْلَمُ مَا بَيْنَ أَيْدِيهِمْ وَمَا خَلْفَهُمْ ۖ وَلَا يُحِيطُونَ بِشَيْءٍ مِنْ عِلْمِهِ إِلَّا بِمَا شَاءَ ۚ وَسِعَ كُرْسِيُّهُ السَّمَاوَاتِ وَالْأَرْضَ ۖ وَلَا يَئُودُهُ حِفْظُهُمَا ۚ وَهُوَ الْعَلِيُّ الْعَظِيمُ ﴿٢٥٥﴾ ﴿البقرة﴾

God - there is no god but Him, the Ever-Living, the Self-Subsistent. Neither slumber overtakes Him nor sleep. Unto Him belongs all that is in the heavens and all that is on the earth. Who is there that could intercede with Him save by His leave? He knows what is before them and what is behind them, and they encompass nothing of His knowledge save what He wills. His Throne extends over the heavens and the earth, and He is never weary of preserving them. And He is the Exalted, the Tremendous (255)

Al-Baqarah (The Cow) 2:255

لَا إِكْرَاهَ فِي الدِّينِ ۔ قَد تَبَيَّنَ الرُّشْدُ مِنَ الْغَيِّ ۔ فَمَنْ يَكْفُرْ بِالطَّاغُوتِ وَيُؤْمِنْ بِاللَّهِ فَقَدِ اسْتَمْسَكَ بِالْعُرْوَةِ الْوُثْقَىٰ لَا انْفِصَامَ لَهَا ۔ وَاللَّهُ سَمِيعٌ عَلِيمٌ ﴿٢٥٦﴾ ﴿البقرة﴾

There is no compulsion in religion. True judgement has become distinct from error. So whoever rejects false gods and believes in God has truly grasped the firmest hand-hold which will never break. God is All-Hearing, All-Knowing (256)

Al-Baqarah (The Cow) 2:256

اللَّهُ وَلِيُّ الَّذِينَ آمَنُوا يُخْرِجُهُمْ مِنَ الظُّلُمَاتِ إِلَى النُّورِ ۖ وَالَّذِينَ كَفَرُوا أَوْلِيَاؤُهُمُ الطَّاغُوتُ يُخْرِجُونَهُمْ مِنَ النُّورِ إِلَى الظُّلُمَاتِ ۗ أُولَٰئِكَ أَصْحَابُ النَّارِ ۖ هُمْ فِيهَا خَالِدُونَ ﴿٢٥٧﴾ ﴿البقرة﴾

God is the Protector of those who believe. He brings them out of the darkness into the light. As for those who disbelieve, their protectors are false gods. They bring them out of the light into the depths of darkness. They are the inhabitants of the Fire, therein they shall abide (257)

Al-Baqarah (The Cow) 2:257

مَثَلُ الَّذِينَ يُنْفِقُونَ أَمْوَالَهُمْ فِي سَبِيلِ اللَّهِ كَمَثَلِ حَبَّةٍ أَنْبَتَتْ سَبْعَ سَنَابِلَ فِي كُلِّ سُنْبُلَةٍ مِائَةُ حَبَّةٍ ۗ وَاللَّهُ يُضَاعِفُ لِمَنْ يَشَاءُ ۚ وَاللَّهُ وَاسِعٌ عَلِيمٌ ﴿٢٦١﴾ ﴿البقرة﴾

The parable of those who spend their wealth in God's cause, is that of a grain that sprouts seven ears, in every ear a hundred grains, for God multiplies unto whom He will and God is Infinite, Knowing (261)

Al-Baqarah (The Cow) 2:261

الَّذِينَ يُنفِقُونَ أَمْوَالَهُمْ فِي سَبِيلِ اللَّهِ ثُمَّ لَا يُتْبِعُونَ مَا أَنْفَقُوا مَنًّا وَلَا أَذًى ۙ لَهُمْ أَجْرُهُمْ عِنْدَ رَبِّهِمْ وَلَا خَوْفٌ عَلَيْهِمْ وَلَا هُمْ يَحْزَنُونَ ﴿٢٦٢﴾ ﴿البقرة﴾

Those who spend their wealth in God's cause and make no reproach on what they spent with reminders of their benevolence or injury shall have their reward with their Lord, and no fear shall come upon them, nor shall they grieve (262)

Al-Baqarah (The Cow) 2:262

قَوْلٌ مَعْرُوفٌ وَمَغْفِرَةٌ خَيْرٌ مِنْ صَدَقَةٍ يَتْبَعُهَا أَذًى ۘ وَاللَّهُ غَنِيٌّ حَلِيمٌ ﴿٢٦٣﴾ ﴿البقرة﴾

A kind word and forgiveness is better than a charitable deed followed by harm. And God is Self-Sufficient, Forbearing (263)

Al-Baqarah (The Cow) 2:263

الشَّيْطَانُ يَعِدُكُمُ الْفَقْرَ وَيَأْمُرُكُم بِالْفَحْشَاءِۖوَاللَّهُ يَعِدُكُم مَغْفِرَةً مِنْهُ وَفَضْلًا ۗ
وَاللَّهُ وَاسِعٌ عَلِيمٌ ﴿٢٦٨﴾ ﴿البقرة﴾

Satan threatens you with the prospect of poverty and commands you to wickedness; God promises you forgiveness from Him, and abundance. And God is Infinite, Knowing (268)

Al-Baqarah (The Cow) 2:268

يُؤْتِي الْحِكْمَةَ مَنْ يَشَاءُ ۚ وَمَنْ يُؤْتَ الْحِكْمَةَ فَقَدْ أُوتِيَ خَيْرًا كَثِيرًا ۚ وَمَا يَذَّكَّرُ إِلَّا أُولُو الْأَلْبَابِ ﴿٢٦٩﴾ ﴿البقرة﴾

He grants wisdom to whomever He will, and he who is granted wisdom, has certainly been granted much good. Yet none remember save those who possess intellect (269)

Al-Baqarah (The Cow) 2:269

وَمَا أَنْفَقْتُم مِنْ نَفَقَةٍ أَوْ نَذَرْتُم مِنْ نَذْرٍ فَإِنَّ اللَّهَ يَعْلَمُهُ ۗ وَمَا لِلظَّالِمِينَ مِنْ

أَنْصَارٍ ﴿٢٧٠﴾ ﴿البقرة﴾

And whatever you spend (in charity), or vow you vow, truly God knows it. And for the wrongdoers there are no helpers (270)

Al-Baqarah (The Cow) 2:270

إِنْ تُبْدُوا الصَّدَقَاتِ فَنِعِمَّا هِيَ ۖ وَإِنْ تُخْفُوهَا وَتُؤْتُوهَا الْفُقَرَاءَ فَهُوَ خَيْرٌ لَكُمْ ۚ وَيُكَفِّرُ عَنْكُمْ مِنْ سَيِّئَاتِكُمْ ۗ وَاللَّهُ بِمَا تَعْمَلُونَ خَبِيرٌ ﴿٢٧١﴾ ﴿البقرة﴾

If you give charity openly, that is well. But if you bestow it upon the poor in secret it will be better for you and it will atone for some of your ill deeds. And God is aware of all that you do (271)

Al-Baqarah (The Cow) 2:271

لَيْسَ عَلَيْكَ هُدَاهُمْ وَلَكِنَّ اللَّهَ يَهْدِي مَنْ يَشَاءُ ۚ وَمَا تُنْفِقُوا مِنْ خَيْرٍ

فَلِأَنْفُسِكُمْ ۚ وَمَا تُنْفِقُونَ إِلَّا ابْتِغَاءَ وَجْهِ اللَّهِ ۚ وَمَا تُنْفِقُوا مِنْ خَيْرٍ يُوَفَّ إِلَيْكُمْ

وَأَنْتُمْ لَا تُظْلَمُونَ ﴿٢٧٢﴾ ﴿البقرة﴾

It is not for thee (Muhammad) to guide them, but God guides whom He will. And whatever good you spend (on others) it is for your own souls, provided you spend only seeking God's countenance; for whatever good you spend will be repaid to you in full, and you shall not be wronged (272)

Al-Baqarah (The Cow) 2:272

لِلْفُقَرَاءِ الَّذِينَ أُحْصِرُوا فِي سَبِيلِ اللَّهِ لَا يَسْتَطِيعُونَ ضَرْبًا فِي الْأَرْضِ يَحْسَبُهُمُ الْجَاهِلُ أَغْنِيَاءَ مِنَ التَّعَفُّفِ تَعْرِفُهُم بِسِيمَاهُمْ لَا يَسْأَلُونَ النَّاسَ إِلْحَافًا ۗ وَمَا تُنْفِقُوا مِنْ خَيْرٍ فَإِنَّ اللَّهَ بِهِ عَلِيمٌ ﴿٢٧٣﴾ ﴿البقرة﴾

(Give) to the poor who are constrained in the cause of God, who cannot move about in the land (for trade). The ignorant might think them wealthy because of their restraint. You recognize them by their mark: they do not beg of men persistently. And whatever good you may spend, truly God knows it (273)

Al-Baqarah (The Cow) 2:273

الَّذِينَ يُنفِقُونَ أَمْوَالَهُم بِاللَّيْلِ وَالنَّهَارِ سِرًّا وَعَلَانِيَةً فَلَهُمْ أَجْرُهُمْ عِندَ رَبِّهِمْ وَلَا خَوْفٌ عَلَيْهِمْ وَلَا هُمْ يَحْزَنُونَ ﴿٢٧٤﴾ ﴿البقرة﴾

Those who spend their wealth (in charity) by night and by day, secretly and openly, shall have their reward with their Lord. No fear shall come upon them, nor shall they grieve (274)

Al-Baqarah (The Cow) 2:274

إِنَّ الَّذِينَ آمَنُوا وَعَمِلُوا الصَّالِحَاتِ وَأَقَامُوا الصَّلَاةَ وَآتَوُا الزَّكَاةَ لَهُمْ أَجْرُهُمْ

عِنْدَ رَبِّهِمْ وَلَا خَوْفٌ عَلَيْهِمْ وَلَا هُمْ يَحْزَنُونَ ﴿٢٧٧﴾ ﴿البقرة﴾

Truly those who believe, perform righteous deeds, are steadfast in prayer, and give the alms, shall have their reward with their Lord. No fear shall come upon them, nor shall they grieve (277)

Al-Baqarah (The Cow) 2:277

آمَنَ الرَّسُولُ بِمَا أُنْزِلَ إِلَيْهِ مِنْ رَبِّهِ وَالْمُؤْمِنُونَ ۚ كُلٌّ آمَنَ بِاللَّهِ وَمَلَائِكَتِهِ وَكُتُبِهِ وَرُسُلِهِ لَا نُفَرِّقُ بَيْنَ أَحَدٍ مِنْ رُسُلِهِ ۚ وَقَالُوا سَمِعْنَا وَأَطَعْنَا ۖ غُفْرَانَكَ رَبَّنَا وَإِلَيْكَ الْمَصِيرُ ﴿٢٨٥﴾ ﴿البقرة﴾

The Messenger believes in what has been sent down unto him from his Lord, as do the believers. They all believe in God and His angels, and in His scriptures, and in His messengers, "We make no distinction between any of His messengers". And they say, "We have heard and have obeyed; grant us Your forgiveness our Lord! And unto Thee is the journey's end" (285)

Al-Baqarah (The Cow) 2:285

لَا يُكَلِّفُ اللَّهُ نَفْسًا إِلَّا وُسْعَهَا ۚ لَهَا مَا كَسَبَتْ وَعَلَيْهَا مَا اكْتَسَبَتْ ۗ رَبَّنَا

لَا تُؤَاخِذْنَا إِنْ نَسِينَا أَوْ أَخْطَأْنَا ۚ رَبَّنَا وَلَا تَحْمِلْ عَلَيْنَا إِصْرًا كَمَا حَمَلْتَهُ

عَلَى الَّذِينَ مِنْ قَبْلِنَا ۚ رَبَّنَا وَلَا تُحَمِّلْنَا مَا لَا طَاقَةَ لَنَا بِهِ ۖ وَاعْفُ عَنَّا وَاغْفِرْ

لَنَا وَارْحَمْنَا ۚ أَنْتَ مَوْلَانَا فَانْصُرْنَا عَلَى الْقَوْمِ الْكَافِرِينَ ﴿٢٨٦﴾ ﴿البقرة﴾

God burdens no soul beyond what it can bear. It shall have what it has earned (from good deeds) and against it what it deserves (from bad deeds). "Our Lord! Condemn us not if we forget or fall in error! Our Lord! Lay not upon us a burden such as Thou laid upon those before us! Our Lord! Make us not bear burdens which we have no strength to bear! Pardon us, forgive us, and have mercy upon us! Thou art our Protector, so help us against the disbelieving people" (286)

Al-Baqarah (The Cow) 2:286

الم ﴿١﴾ اللَّهُ لَا إِلَٰهَ إِلَّا هُوَ الْحَيُّ الْقَيُّومُ ﴿٢﴾ نَزَّلَ عَلَيْكَ الْكِتَابَ بِالْحَقِّ

مُصَدِّقًا لِمَا بَيْنَ يَدَيْهِ وَأَنْزَلَ التَّوْرَاةَ وَالْإِنْجِيلَ ﴿٣﴾ ﴿آل عمران﴾

Alif. Lām. Mīm (1) God - there is no god but Him, the Ever-Living, the Self-Subsistent (2) He sent down the Scripture upon thee in truth, confirming what was sent down before it (of earlier revelations), and He sent down the Torah and the Gospel (3)

Al-Imrān (The Family of Imran) 3:1-3

إِنَّ اللَّهَ لَا يَخْفَىٰ عَلَيْهِ شَيْءٌ فِي الْأَرْضِ وَلَا فِي السَّمَاءِ ﴿٥﴾ ﴿آلعمران﴾

Truly nothing in the earth or in the heavens is hidden from God (5)

Al-Imrān (The Family of Imran) 3:5

هُوَ الَّذِي يُصَوِّرُكُمْ فِي الْأَرْحَامِ كَيْفَ يَشَاءُ ۚ لَا إِلَٰهَ إِلَّا هُوَ الْعَزِيزُ الْحَكِيمُ ﴿٦﴾ ﴿آلعمران﴾

It is He Who shapes you in the wombs as He wills. There is no God but Him, the Almighty, the Wise (6)

Al-Imrān (The Family of Imran) 3:6

رَبَّنَا لَا تُزِغْ قُلُوبَنَا بَعْدَ إِذْ هَدَيْتَنَا وَهَبْ لَنَا مِنْ لَدُنْكَ رَحْمَةً ۚ إِنَّكَ أَنْتَ الْوَهَّابُ ﴿٨﴾ ﴿آلعمران﴾

"Our Lord, let not our hearts swerve (from the truth) after you have guided us, and bestow upon us a mercy from Thy Presence. Thou art the Bestower" (8)

Al-Imrān (The Family of Imran) 3:8

رَبَّنَا إِنَّكَ جَامِعُ النَّاسِ لِيَوْمٍ لَا رَيْبَ فِيهِ إِنَّ اللَّهَ لَا يُخْلِفُ الْمِيعَادَ ﴿٩﴾ ﴿آل عمران﴾

"Our Lord, truly Thou shall gather mankind unto a Day about which (the coming of) there is no doubt. Truly God never fails to fulfill His promise" (9)

Al-Imrān (The Family of Imran) 3:9

قُلِ اللَّهُمَّ مَالِكَ الْمُلْكِ تُؤْتِي الْمُلْكَ مَنْ تَشَاءُ وَتَنْزِعُ الْمُلْكَ مِمَّنْ تَشَاءُ وَتُعِزُّ
مَنْ تَشَاءُ وَتُذِلُّ مَنْ تَشَاءُ بِيَدِكَ الْخَيْرُ إِنَّكَ عَلَىٰ كُلِّ شَيْءٍ قَدِيرٌ ﴿٢٦﴾
﴿آل عمران﴾

Say "O God, Master of Sovereignty. You give authority unto whom You will, and You withdraw authority from whom You will. You elevate whom You will and humble whom You will. In Your hand is all good. Truly You are Powerful over all things" (26)

Al-Imrān (The Family of Imran) 3:26

تُولِجُ اللَّيْلَ فِي النَّهَارِ وَتُولِجُ النَّهَارَ فِي اللَّيْلِ ـ وَتُخْرِجُ الْحَيَّ مِنَ الْمَيِّتِ وَتُخْرِجُ الْمَيِّتَ مِنَ الْحَيِّ ـ وَتَرْزُقُ مَنْ تَشَاءُ بِغَيْرِ حِسَابٍ ﴿٢٧﴾ ﴿آل عمران﴾

"You cause the night to pass into the day, and You cause the day to pass into the night. You bring forth the living from the dead, and You bring forth the dead from the living. And You grant sustenance unto whom You will without reckoning" (27)

Al-Imrān (The Family of Imran) 3:27

يَوْمَ تَجِدُ كُلُّ نَفْسٍ مَا عَمِلَتْ مِنْ خَيْرٍ مُحْضَرًا وَمَا عَمِلَتْ مِنْ سُوءٍ تَوَدُّ

لَوْ أَنَّ بَيْنَهَا وَبَيْنَهُ أَمَدًا بَعِيدًا ۗ وَيُحَذِّرُكُمُ اللَّهُ نَفْسَهُ ۗ وَاللَّهُ رَءُوفٌ بِالْعِبَادِ

﴿٣٠﴾ ﴿آل عمران﴾

On the Day when every soul finds itself confronted with all the good it has done and all the evil it has done (every soul) will wish there were a great distance between it and its evil. And God warns you to beware of Him; and God is most Compassionate towards His servants (30)

Al-Imrān (The Family of Imran) 3:30

قُلْ إِنْ كُنْتُمْ تُحِبُّونَ اللَّهَ فَاتَّبِعُونِي يُحْبِبْكُمُ اللَّهُ وَيَغْفِرْ لَكُمْ ذُنُوبَكُمْ ۚ وَاللَّهُ غَفُورٌ رَحِيمٌ ﴿٣١﴾ ﴿آلعمران﴾

Say, (O Muhammad) "If you love God, then follow me; God will love you and forgive you your sins. And God is Forgiving, Merciful" (31)

Al-Imrān (The Family of Imran) 3:31

يَا أَيُّهَا الَّذِينَ آمَنُوا اتَّقُوا اللَّهَ حَقَّ تُقَاتِهِ وَلَا تَمُوتُنَّ إِلَّا وَأَنْتُمْ مُسْلِمُونَ
﴿١٠٢﴾ ﴿آلعمران﴾

O you who believe! Be conscious of God with all the consciousness that is due to Him, and die not except in submission (102)

Al-Imrān (The Family of Imran) 3:102

وَاعْتَصِمُوا بِحَبْلِ اللَّهِ جَمِيعًا وَلَا تَفَرَّقُوا ۚ وَاذْكُرُوا نِعْمَتَ اللَّهِ عَلَيْكُمْ إِذْ

كُنْتُمْ أَعْدَاءً فَأَلَّفَ بَيْنَ قُلُوبِكُمْ فَأَصْبَحْتُمْ بِنِعْمَتِهِ إِخْوَانًا وَكُنْتُمْ عَلَىٰ شَفَا

حُفْرَةٍ مِنَ النَّارِ فَأَنْقَذَكُمْ مِنْهَا ۗ كَذَٰلِكَ يُبَيِّنُ اللَّهُ لَكُمْ آيَاتِهِ لَعَلَّكُمْ تَهْتَدُونَ

﴿١٠٣﴾ ﴿آل عمران﴾

And hold fast, all together, to God's rope, and be not divided (from one another). And remember the blessings which God bestowed upon you, how when you were enemies, He brought your hearts together so that through His grace you became as brothers. And how when you were on the brink of the pit of fire, He saved you from it. Thus, God makes clear His revelations to you, so that you may be rightly guided (103)

Al-Imrān (The Family of Imran) 3:103

لَيْسُوا سَوَاءً مِنْ أَهْلِ الْكِتَابِ أُمَّةٌ قَائِمَةٌ يَتْلُونَ آيَاتِ اللَّهِ آنَاءَ اللَّيْلِ وَهُمْ

يَسْجُدُونَ ﴿١١٣﴾ يُؤْمِنُونَ بِاللَّهِ وَالْيَوْمِ الْآخِرِ وَيَأْمُرُونَ بِالْمَعْرُوفِ وَيَنْهَوْنَ

عَنِ الْمُنْكَرِ وَيُسَارِعُونَ فِي الْخَيْرَاتِ وَأُولَٰئِكَ مِنَ الصَّالِحِينَ ﴿١١٤﴾ وَمَا

يَفْعَلُوا مِنْ خَيْرٍ فَلَنْ يُكْفَرُوهُ ۗ وَاللَّهُ عَلِيمٌ بِالْمُتَّقِينَ ﴿١١٥﴾ ﴿آلعمران﴾

They are not all alike. Among the People of the Scripture is an
upright community who recite God's verses during the night while
they prostrate (before Him) (113) They believe in God and the Last
Day, and order what is right and forbid what is wrong and hasten
unto good deeds and they are among the righteous (114) And whatever good they do, they will not be denied (the reward): for God has
full knowledge of those who are conscious of Him (115)

Al-Imrān (The Family of Imran) 3:113-115

وَسَارِعُوا إِلَىٰ مَغْفِرَةٍ مِنْ رَبِّكُمْ وَجَنَّةٍ عَرْضُهَا السَّمَاوَاتُ وَالْأَرْضُ أُعِدَّتْ

لِلْمُتَّقِينَ ﴿١٣٣﴾ ﴿آلعمران﴾

And hasten unto forgiveness from your Lord, and to a paradise as wide as the heavens and the earth, which has been prepared for the God-conscious (133)

Al-Imrān (The Family of Imran) 3:133

الَّذِينَ يُنْفِقُونَ فِي السَّرَّاءِ وَالضَّرَّاءِ وَالْكَاظِمِينَ الْغَيْظَ وَالْعَافِينَ عَنِ النَّاسِ ۗ وَاللَّهُ يُحِبُّ الْمُحْسِنِينَ ﴿١٣٤﴾ ﴿آل عمران﴾

Who spend in prosperity and adversity, and curb their rage, and pardon people – and God loves the virtuous (134)

Al-Imrān (The Family of Imran) 3:134

وَالَّذِينَ إِذَا فَعَلُوا فَاحِشَةً أَوْ ظَلَمُوا أَنْفُسَهُمْ ذَكَرُوا اللَّهَ فَاسْتَغْفَرُوا لِذُنُوبِهِمْ وَمَنْ يَغْفِرُ الذُّنُوبَ إِلَّا اللَّهُ وَلَمْ يُصِرُّوا عَلَىٰ مَا فَعَلُوا وَهُمْ يَعْلَمُونَ ﴿١٣٥﴾ أُولَٰئِكَ جَزَاؤُهُمْ مَغْفِرَةٌ مِنْ رَبِّهِمْ وَجَنَّاتٌ تَجْرِي مِنْ تَحْتِهَا الْأَنْهَارُ خَالِدِينَ فِيهَا ۚ وَنِعْمَ أَجْرُ الْعَامِلِينَ ﴿١٣٦﴾ ﴿آل عمران﴾

And who when they commit an indecency or wrong themselves remember God and ask forgiveness for their sins - and who forgives sins but God? And who do not knowingly persist in doing whatever (wrong) they have done (135) For those, their reward is forgiveness from their Lord, and Gardens beneath which rivers flow, abiding therein. And how excellent is the reward of those who labour (136)

Al-Imrān (The Family of Imran) 3:135-136

وَلَا تَهِنُوا وَلَا تَحْزَنُوا وَأَنْتُمُ الْأَعْلَوْنَ إِنْ كُنْتُمْ مُؤْمِنِينَ ﴿١٣٩﴾ ﴿آلعمران﴾

Do not lose heart and do not despair, for you will rise high if you are believers (139)

Al-Imrān (The Family of Imran) 3:139

إِنَّ فِي خَلْقِ السَّمَاوَاتِ وَالْأَرْضِ وَاخْتِلَافِ اللَّيْلِ وَالنَّهَارِ لَآيَاتٍ لِأُولِي

الْأَلْبَابِ ﴿١٩٠﴾ الَّذِينَ يَذْكُرُونَ اللَّهَ قِيَامًا وَقُعُودًا وَعَلَىٰ جُنُوبِهِمْ وَيَتَفَكَّرُونَ

فِي خَلْقِ السَّمَاوَاتِ وَالْأَرْضِ رَبَّنَا مَا خَلَقْتَ هَٰذَا بَاطِلًا سُبْحَانَكَ فَقِنَا

عَذَابَ النَّارِ ﴿١٩١﴾ ﴿آلعمران﴾

Indeed in the creation of the heavens and the earth, and in the alternation of night and day, are signs for the possessors of intellect (190) Who remember God while standing and sitting and lying on their sides, and contemplate upon the creation of the heavens and the earth, "Our Lord, Thou hast not created this without purpose. Glory to Thee! So protect us from the punishment of the Fire" (191)

Al-Imrān (The Family of Imran) 3:190-191

رَبَّنَا إِنَّكَ مَنْ تُدْخِلِ النَّارَ فَقَدْ أَخْزَيْتَهُ وَمَا لِلظَّالِمِينَ مِنْ أَنْصَارٍ ﴿١٩٢﴾

﴿آل عمران﴾

"Our Lord! Whomever Thou shall commit to the Fire, Thou hast surely disgraced him. And for the wrongdoers there are no helpers" (192)

Al-Imrān (The Family of Imran) 3:192

رَبَّنَا إِنَّنَا سَمِعْنَا مُنَادِيًا يُنَادِي لِلْإِيمَانِ أَنْ آمِنُوا بِرَبِّكُمْ فَآمَنَّا ۚ رَبَّنَا فَاغْفِرْ لَنَا

ذُنُوبَنَا وَكَفِّرْ عَنَّا سَيِّئَاتِنَا وَتَوَفَّنَا مَعَ الْأَبْرَارِ ﴿١٩٣﴾ ﴿آلعمران﴾

"Our Lord! We have heard a caller calling us to faith, saying 'Believe in your Lord' so we believed. Our Lord, then forgive us our sins and absolve us of our evil deeds, and when we die join our souls with the pious" (193)

Al-Imrān (The Family of Imran) 3:193

رَبَّنَا وَآتِنَا مَا وَعَدتَنَا عَلَىٰ رُسُلِكَ وَلَا تُخْزِنَا يَوْمَ الْقِيَامَةِ ۖ إِنَّكَ لَا تُخْلِفُ الْمِيعَادَ ﴿١٩٤﴾ ﴿آل عمران﴾

"Our Lord! Grant us what Thou hast promised us through Thy messengers, and do not disgrace us on the Day of Resurrection. Truly Thou never breakest the tryst" (194)

Al-Imrān (The Family of Imran) 3:194

لٰكِنِ الَّذِينَ اتَّقَوْا رَبَّهُمْ لَهُمْ جَنَّاتٌ تَجْرِي مِنْ تَحْتِهَا الْأَنْهَارُ خَالِدِينَ فِيهَا
نُزُلًا مِنْ عِنْدِ اللَّهِ ۗ وَمَا عِنْدَ اللَّهِ خَيْرٌ لِلْأَبْرَارِ ﴿١٩٨﴾ ﴿آلعمران﴾

But those who remained conscious of their Lord shall have Gardens beneath which rivers flow, abiding therein; a gift of welcome from God. And that which is from God is best for the pious (198)

Al-Imrān (The Family of Imran) 3:198

وَإِنَّ مِنْ أَهْلِ الْكِتَابِ لَمَنْ يُؤْمِنُ بِاللَّهِ وَمَا أُنْزِلَ إِلَيْكُمْ وَمَا أُنْزِلَ إِلَيْهِمْ خَاشِعِينَ لِلَّهِ لَا يَشْتَرُونَ بِآيَاتِ اللَّهِ ثَمَنًا قَلِيلًا ۚ أُولَٰئِكَ لَهُمْ أَجْرُهُمْ عِنْدَ رَبِّهِمْ ۗ إِنَّ اللَّهَ سَرِيعُ الْحِسَابِ ﴿١٩٩﴾ ﴿آل عمران﴾

And truly among the People of the Scripture are some who believe in God and what was sent down to you and what was sent down to them, humble before God, they do not barter away God's messages for a trifling gain. It is they who shall have their reward with their Lord. Truly God is swift in reckoning (199)

Al-Imrān (The Family of Imran) 3:199

يَا أَيُّهَا الَّذِينَ آمَنُوا اصْبِرُوا وَصَابِرُوا وَرَابِطُوا وَاتَّقُوا اللَّهَ لَعَلَّكُمْ تُفْلِحُونَ

﴿٢٠٠﴾ ﴿آلعمران﴾

O you who believe! Be patient and vie in patience and be ready and be mindful of God, so that you may prosper (200)

Al-Imrān (The Family of Imran) 3:200

يَا أَيُّهَا النَّاسُ اتَّقُوا رَبَّكُمُ الَّذِي خَلَقَكُمْ مِنْ نَفْسٍ وَاحِدَةٍ وَخَلَقَ مِنْهَا زَوْجَهَا

وَبَثَّ مِنْهُمَا رِجَالًا كَثِيرًا وَنِسَاءً ۚ وَاتَّقُوا اللَّهَ الَّذِي تَسَاءَلُونَ بِهِ وَالْأَرْحَامَ ۚ

إِنَّ اللَّهَ كَانَ عَلَيْكُمْ رَقِيبًا ﴿١﴾ وَآتُوا الْيَتَامَىٰ أَمْوَالَهُمْ ۖ وَلَا تَتَبَدَّلُوا الْخَبِيثَ

بِالطَّيِّبِ ۖ وَلَا تَأْكُلُوا أَمْوَالَهُمْ إِلَىٰ أَمْوَالِكُمْ ۚ إِنَّهُ كَانَ حُوبًا كَبِيرًا ﴿٢﴾

﴿النساء﴾

O mankind! Be conscious of your Lord, who created you from a single
soul and from it created its mate, and from the two has spread abroad
a multitude of men and women. Be mindful of God, in whose name
you claim (your rights) from one another and kinship ties. Truly God
is ever watchful over you (1) And give the orphans their wealth, and
do not exchange the bad for the good, nor consume their wealth with
your own. Indeed, that is a great sin (2)

Al-Nisā (The Women) 4:1-2

يَا أَيُّهَا الَّذِينَ آمَنُوا لَا يَحِلُّ لَكُمْ أَنْ تَرِثُوا النِّسَاءَ كَرْهًا ۔ وَلَا تَعْضُلُوهُنَّ
لِتَذْهَبُوا بِبَعْضِ مَا آتَيْتُمُوهُنَّ إِلَّا أَنْ يَأْتِينَ بِفَاحِشَةٍ مُبَيِّنَةٍ ۔ وَعَاشِرُوهُنَّ
بِالْمَعْرُوفِ ۔ فَإِنْ كَرِهْتُمُوهُنَّ فَعَسَىٰ أَنْ تَكْرَهُوا شَيْئًا وَيَجْعَلَ اللَّهُ فِيهِ خَيْرًا
كَثِيرًا ﴿١٩﴾ ﴿النساء﴾

O you who believe! It is unlawful for you to inherit women against their will, nor should you treat them (your wives) with harshness so that you may go off with part of what you have given them, unless they commit a blatant indecency. And live with them in kindness and if you dislike them, it may be that you dislike something in which God has placed much good (19)

Al-Nisā (The Women) 4:19

وَاللَّهُ يُرِيدُ أَنْ يَتُوبَ عَلَيْكُمْ وَيُرِيدُ الَّذِينَ يَتَّبِعُونَ الشَّهَوَاتِ أَنْ تَمِيلُوا مَيْلًا

عَظِيمًا ﴿٢٧﴾ ﴿النساء﴾

God wants to turn to you, but those who follow their lusts want you to drift tremendously astray (27)

Al-Nisā (The Women) 4:27

يُرِيدُ اللَّهُ أَنْ يُخَفِّفَ عَنْكُمْ ۚ وَخُلِقَ الْإِنْسَانُ ضَعِيفًا ﴿٢٨﴾ ﴿النساء﴾

God wants to lighten your burden; for man was created weak (28)

Al-Nisā (The Women) 4:28

يَا أَيُّهَا الَّذِينَ آمَنُوا لَا تَأْكُلُوا أَمْوَالَكُمْ بَيْنَكُمْ بِالْبَاطِلِ إِلَّا أَنْ تَكُونَ تِجَارَةً عَنْ تَرَاضٍ مِنْكُمْ ، وَلَا تَقْتُلُوا أَنْفُسَكُمْ ، إِنَّ اللَّهَ كَانَ بِكُمْ رَحِيمًا ﴿٢٩﴾ ﴿النساء﴾

O you who believe! Do not consume each other's wealth wrongfully, but rather trade by mutual consent, and do not kill one another. Truly God is Merciful unto you (29)

Al-Nisā (The Women) 4:29

وَاعْبُدُوا اللَّهَ وَلَا تُشْرِكُوا بِهِ شَيْئًا ۖ وَبِالْوَالِدَيْنِ إِحْسَانًا وَبِذِي الْقُرْبَىٰ وَالْيَتَامَىٰ وَالْمَسَاكِينِ وَالْجَارِ ذِي الْقُرْبَىٰ وَالْجَارِ الْجُنُبِ وَالصَّاحِبِ بِالْجَنْبِ وَابْنِ السَّبِيلِ وَمَا مَلَكَتْ أَيْمَانُكُمْ ۗ إِنَّ اللَّهَ لَا يُحِبُّ مَنْ كَانَ مُخْتَالًا فَخُورًا ﴿٣٦﴾ ﴿النساء﴾

And worship God and join nothing with Him. And be virtuous to your parents, and near of kin, and to orphans and the needy, and the neighbour who is of kin, and the neighbour who is a stranger, and the friend by your side, and the wayfarer, and those whom your right hand possess. Truly God does not love the arrogant and the boastful (36)

Al-Nisā (The Women) 4:36

وَالَّذِينَ آمَنُوا وَعَمِلُوا الصَّالِحَاتِ سَنُدْخِلُهُمْ جَنَّاتٍ تَجْرِي مِنْ تَحْتِهَا الْأَنْهَارُ خَالِدِينَ فِيهَا أَبَدًا ۔ لَهُمْ فِيهَا أَزْوَاجٌ مُطَهَّرَةٌ ۔ وَنُدْخِلُهُمْ ظِلًّا ظَلِيلًا ﴿٥٧﴾ ﴿النساء﴾

As for those who believe and perform righteous deeds, We shall admit them into Gardens beneath which rivers flow, abiding therein forever. There they shall have spouses made pure, and We shall admit them into bountiful shade (57)

Al-Nisā (The Women) 4:57

إِنَّ اللَّهَ يَأْمُرُكُمْ أَنْ تُؤَدُّوا الْأَمَانَاتِ إِلَى أَهْلِهَا وَإِذَا حَكَمْتُمْ بَيْنَ النَّاسِ أَنْ تَحْكُمُوا بِالْعَدْلِ ۚ إِنَّ اللَّهَ نِعِمَّا يَعِظُكُمْ بِهِ ۗ إِنَّ اللَّهَ كَانَ سَمِيعًا بَصِيرًا ﴿٥٨﴾ ﴿النساء﴾

Truly God commands you to return the trusts to their owners, and when you judge between people, to judge with justice. Excellent indeed is the instruction God gives you. Truly God is Hearing, Seeing (58)

Al-Nisā (The Women) 4:58

يَا أَيُّهَا الَّذِينَ آمَنُوا أَطِيعُوا اللَّهَ وَأَطِيعُوا الرَّسُولَ وَأُولِي الْأَمْرِ مِنْكُمْ ۖ فَإِنْ تَنَازَعْتُمْ فِي شَيْءٍ فَرُدُّوهُ إِلَى اللَّهِ وَالرَّسُولِ إِنْ كُنْتُمْ تُؤْمِنُونَ بِاللَّهِ وَالْيَوْمِ الْآخِرِ ۚ ذَٰلِكَ خَيْرٌ وَأَحْسَنُ تَأْوِيلًا ﴿٥٩﴾ ﴿النساء﴾

O you who believe! Obey God and obey the Messenger and those in authority among you. And if you dispute over any matter, refer it to God and the Messenger, if you believe in God and the Last Day. That is best, and fairer in the end (59)

Al-Nisā (The Women) 4:59

وَمَنْ يُطِعِ اللَّهَ وَالرَّسُولَ فَأُولَٰئِكَ مَعَ الَّذِينَ أَنْعَمَ اللَّهُ عَلَيْهِمْ مِنَ النَّبِيِّينَ وَالصِّدِّيقِينَ وَالشُّهَدَاءِ وَالصَّالِحِينَ ۚ وَحَسُنَ أُولَٰئِكَ رَفِيقًا ﴿٦٩﴾ ﴿النساء﴾

Whoever obeys God and the Messenger, are among those on whom God has blessed of the prophets and the truthful, the martyrs and the righteous. What excellent companions they are (69)

Al-Nisā (The Women) 4:69

فَإِذَا قَضَيْتُمُ الصَّلَاةَ فَاذْكُرُوا اللَّهَ قِيَامًا وَقُعُودًا وَعَلَىٰ جُنُوبِكُمْ ۚ فَإِذَا اطْمَأْنَنْتُمْ

فَأَقِيمُوا الصَّلَاةَ ۚ إِنَّ الصَّلَاةَ كَانَتْ عَلَى الْمُؤْمِنِينَ كِتَابًا مَوْقُوتًا ﴿١٠٣﴾

﴿النساء﴾

When you have completed the prayer, remember God, standing, sitting and lying on your sides. And when you are safe (once again), observe regular prayer, for prayer is prescribed for the believers at fixed times (103)

Al-Nisā (The Women) 4:103

إِنَّا أَنْزَلْنَا إِلَيْكَ الْكِتَابَ بِالْحَقِّ لِتَحْكُمَ بَيْنَ النَّاسِ بِمَا أَرَاكَ اللَّهُ ۚ وَلَا تَكُنْ

لِلْخَائِنِينَ خَصِيمًا ﴿١٠٥﴾ وَاسْتَغْفِرِ اللَّهَ ۖ إِنَّ اللَّهَ كَانَ غَفُورًا رَحِيمًا ﴿١٠٦﴾

وَلَا تُجَادِلْ عَنِ الَّذِينَ يَخْتَانُونَ أَنْفُسَهُمْ ۚ إِنَّ اللَّهَ لَا يُحِبُّ مَنْ كَانَ خَوَّانًا

أَثِيمًا ﴿١٠٧﴾ ﴿النساء﴾

Truly We have sent down the Scripture onto you in truth, so that you may judge between people in accordance with what God has shown you. So do not be an advocate for those who betray trust (105) And seek forgiveness of God, truly God is ever Forgiving, Merciful (106) And plead not on behalf of those who betray their own selves, truly God does not love those who give in to treacherous sins (107)

Al-Nisā (The Women) 4:105-107

وَمَن يَعْمَلْ سُوءًا أَوْ يَظْلِمْ نَفْسَهُ ثُمَّ يَسْتَغْفِرِ اللَّهَ يَجِدِ اللَّهَ غَفُورًا رَحِيمًا

﴿١١٠﴾ ﴿النساء﴾

Yet he who does evil or wrongs his own soul and then asks God for forgiveness, he shall find God is Forgiving, Merciful (110)

Al-Nisā (The Women) 4:110

وَمَنْ يَعْمَلْ مِنَ الصَّالِحَاتِ مِنْ ذَكَرٍ أَوْ أُنْثَى وَهُوَ مُؤْمِنٌ فَأُولَٰئِكَ يَدْخُلُونَ الْجَنَّةَ وَلَا يُظْلَمُونَ نَقِيرًا ﴿١٢٤﴾ وَمَنْ أَحْسَنُ دِينًا مِمَّنْ أَسْلَمَ وَجْهَهُ لِلَّهِ وَهُوَ مُحْسِنٌ وَاتَّبَعَ مِلَّةَ إِبْرَاهِيمَ حَنِيفًا ۗ وَاتَّخَذَ اللَّهُ إِبْرَاهِيمَ خَلِيلًا ﴿١٢٥﴾ ﴿النساء﴾

And whoever performs righteous deeds, whether male or female, and is a believer, shall enter paradise, and shall not be wronged by as much as a groove of a date-stone (124) And who better in faith than he who surrenders himself fully to God, and is virtuous, and follows the creed of Abraham, the upright? And God took Abraham for a friend (125)

Al-Nisā (The Women) 4:124-125

وَلِلَّهِ مَا فِي السَّمَاوَاتِ وَمَا فِي الْأَرْضِ ، وَكَانَ اللَّهُ بِكُلِّ شَيْءٍ مُحِيطًا

﴿١٢٦﴾ ﴿النساء﴾

For unto God belongs all that is in the heavens and all that is on earth and God encompasses everything (126)

Al-Nisā (The Women) 4:126

وَلِلَّهِ مَا فِي السَّمَاوَاتِ وَمَا فِي الْأَرْضِ ۚ وَكَفَىٰ بِاللَّهِ وَكِيلًا ﴿١٣٢﴾ ﴿النساء﴾

And unto God belongs all that is in the heavens and all that is on the earth. And God suffices as a Guardian (132)

Al-Nisā (The Women) 4:132

مَنْ كَانَ يُرِيدُ ثَوَابَ الدُّنْيَا فَعِنْدَ اللَّهِ ثَوَابُ الدُّنْيَا وَالْآخِرَةِ ۚ وَكَانَ اللَّهُ سَمِيعًا بَصِيرًا ﴿١٣٤﴾ ﴿النساء﴾

Whoever desires the rewards of this world, with God are the rewards of this world and the Hereafter, and indeed God is Seeing, Hearing (134)

Al-Nisā (The Women) 4:134

يَا أَيُّهَا الَّذِينَ آمَنُوا كُونُوا قَوَّامِينَ بِالْقِسْطِ شُهَدَاءَ لِلَّهِ وَلَوْ عَلَىٰ أَنْفُسِكُمْ
أَوِ الْوَالِدَيْنِ وَالْأَقْرَبِينَ ۚ إِنْ يَكُنْ غَنِيًّا أَوْ فَقِيرًا فَاللَّهُ أَوْلَىٰ بِهِمَا ۖ فَلَا تَتَّبِعُوا
الْهَوَىٰ أَنْ تَعْدِلُوا ۚ وَإِنْ تَلْوُوا أَوْ تُعْرِضُوا فَإِنَّ اللَّهَ كَانَ بِمَا تَعْمَلُونَ خَبِيرًا

﴿١٣٥﴾ ﴿النساء﴾

O you who believe! Be steadfast upholders of justice, witnesses for God,
even if it is against yourselves or your parents and kinsfolk, whether
the person be rich or poor, for God is nearer unto both. Do not follow
your own desires so that you may act justly. And if you distort or refuse
(to act justly) truly God is aware of all that you do (135)

Al-Nisā (The Women) 4:135

يَا أَهْلَ الْكِتَابِ لَا تَغْلُوا فِي دِينِكُمْ وَلَا تَقُولُوا عَلَى اللَّهِ إِلَّا الْحَقَّ ۚ إِنَّمَا

الْمَسِيحُ عِيسَى ابْنُ مَرْيَمَ رَسُولُ اللَّهِ وَكَلِمَتُهُ أَلْقَاهَا إِلَىٰ مَرْيَمَ وَرُوحٌ مِنْهُ ۖ

فَآمِنُوا بِاللَّهِ وَرُسُلِهِ ۖ وَلَا تَقُولُوا ثَلَاثَةٌ ۚ انْتَهُوا خَيْرًا لَكُمْ ۚ إِنَّمَا اللَّهُ إِلَٰهٌ وَاحِدٌ ۖ

سُبْحَانَهُ أَنْ يَكُونَ لَهُ وَلَدٌ ۘ لَهُ مَا فِي السَّمَاوَاتِ وَمَا فِي الْأَرْضِ ۗ وَكَفَىٰ بِاللَّهِ

وَكِيلًا ﴿١٧١﴾ ﴿النساء﴾

O People of the Scripture! Do not exaggerate in your religion and do
not say (anything) about God save the truth. Truly the Messiah, Jesus
son of Mary, was but a messenger of God, and His word which He con-
veyed unto Mary, and a spirit from Him. So believe in God and His messengers, and do not say "Three" (Trinity) – Cease it is better for you; for
God is only One God. Glory be to Him that He should have a child. Unto
Him belongs all that is in the heavens and all that is on the earth. And
God suffices as a Guardian (171)

Al-Nisā (The Women) 4:171

يَا أَيُّهَا النَّاسُ قَدْ جَاءَكُمْ بُرْهَانٌ مِنْ رَبِّكُمْ وَأَنْزَلْنَا إِلَيْكُمْ نُورًا مُبِينًا ﴿١٧٤﴾

﴿النساء﴾

O mankind! Proof has come to you from your Lord, and We have sent down unto you a clear light (174)

Al-Nisā (The Women) 4:174

وَاذْكُرُوا نِعْمَةَ اللَّهِ عَلَيْكُمْ وَمِيثَاقَهُ الَّذِي وَاثَقَكُمْ بِهِ إِذْ قُلْتُمْ سَمِعْنَا وَأَطَعْنَا

وَاتَّقُوا اللَّهَ، إِنَّ اللَّهَ عَلِيمٌ بِذَاتِ الصُّدُورِ ﴿٧﴾ ﴿المائدة﴾

And remember God's blessings upon you, and His pledge by which He bound you with when you said, "We hear and we obey" And be mindful of God. Truly God knows what is in the hearts (7)

Al-Mā'idah (The Feast) 5:7

يَا أَيُّهَا الَّذِينَ آمَنُوا كُونُوا قَوَّامِينَ لِلَّهِ شُهَدَاءَ بِالْقِسْطِ ۖ وَلَا يَجْرِمَنَّكُمْ شَنَآنُ قَوْمٍ عَلَىٰ أَلَّا تَعْدِلُوا ۚ اعْدِلُوا هُوَ أَقْرَبُ لِلتَّقْوَىٰ ۖ وَاتَّقُوا اللَّهَ ۚ إِنَّ اللَّهَ خَبِيرٌ بِمَا تَعْمَلُونَ ﴿٨﴾ ﴿المائدة﴾

O you who believe! Be steadfast in your devotion to God, witnesses in equity, and never let hatred of anyone lead you to be unjust. Be just, that is closest to being God-conscious. And be mindful of God. Truly, God is aware of all that you do (8)

Al-Māʾidah (The Feast) 5:8

وَعَدَ اللَّهُ الَّذِينَ آمَنُوا وَعَمِلُوا الصَّالِحَاتِ ۙ لَهُم مَغْفِرَةٌ وَأَجْرٌ عَظِيمٌ ﴿٩﴾

﴿المائدة﴾

God has promised those who believe and perform righteous deeds, for-giveness and a great reward (9)

Al-Mā'idah (The Feast) 5:9

يَا أَيُّهَا الَّذِينَ آمَنُوا اذْكُرُوا نِعْمَتَ اللَّهِ عَلَيْكُمْ إِذْ هَمَّ قَوْمٌ أَنْ يَبْسُطُوا إِلَيْكُمْ أَيْدِيَهُمْ فَكَفَّ أَيْدِيَهُمْ عَنْكُمْ ۖ وَاتَّقُوا اللَّهَ ۚ وَعَلَى اللَّهِ فَلْيَتَوَكَّلِ الْمُؤْمِنُونَ ﴿١١﴾ ﴿المائدة﴾

O you who believe! Remember God's blessing upon you, when a people were prepared to stretch out their hands against you but He withheld their hands from you. And be mindful of God, and in God let the believers put their trust (11)

Al-Māʾidah (The Feast) 5:11

يَا أَهْلَ الْكِتَابِ قَدْ جَاءَكُمْ رَسُولُنَا يُبَيِّنُ لَكُمْ كَثِيرًا مِمَّا كُنْتُمْ تُخْفُونَ مِنَ

الْكِتَابِ وَيَعْفُو عَنْ كَثِيرٍ ۚ قَدْ جَاءَكُمْ مِنَ اللَّهِ نُورٌ وَكِتَابٌ مُبِينٌ ﴿١٥﴾

يَهْدِي بِهِ اللَّهُ مَنِ اتَّبَعَ رِضْوَانَهُ سُبُلَ السَّلَامِ وَيُخْرِجُهُمْ مِنَ الظُّلُمَاتِ إِلَى

النُّورِ بِإِذْنِهِ وَيَهْدِيهِمْ إِلَىٰ صِرَاطٍ مُسْتَقِيمٍ ﴿١٦﴾ ﴿المائدة﴾

O People of the Scripture! Our Messenger has come unto you making clear to you much of what you have concealed from the Scripture and pardoning much. There has come unto you, from God, a light and a clear Scripture (15) Through which God guides those who seek His good pleasure unto the paths of peace and brings them out of the depths of darkness into the light, by His grace, and guides them onto a straight path (16)

Al-Māʾidah (The Feast) 5:15-16

يَا أَيُّهَا الَّذِينَ آمَنُوا لَا تَتَّخِذُوا الَّذِينَ اتَّخَذُوا دِينَكُمْ هُزُوًا وَلَعِبًا مِنَ الَّذِينَ أُوتُوا الْكِتَابَ مِنْ قَبْلِكُمْ وَالْكُفَّارَ أَوْلِيَاءَ ۚ وَاتَّقُوا اللَّهَ إِنْ كُنْتُمْ مُؤْمِنِينَ ﴿٥٧﴾ ﴿المائدة﴾

O you who believe! Do not take as friends those who take your religion in mockery and jest - whether among those who received the Scripture before you, or disbelievers - and be mindful of God if you are (true) believers (57)

Al-Māʾidah (The Feast) 5:57

لَيْسَ عَلَى الَّذِينَ آمَنُوا وَعَمِلُوا الصَّالِحَاتِ جُنَاحٌ فِيمَا طَعِمُوا إِذَا مَا اتَّقَوْا

وَآمَنُوا وَعَمِلُوا الصَّالِحَاتِ ثُمَّ اتَّقَوْا وَآمَنُوا ثُمَّ اتَّقَوْا ثُمَّ اتَّقَوْا وَأَحْسَنُوا ۚ وَاللَّهُ يُحِبُّ

الْمُحْسِنِينَ ﴿٩٣﴾ ﴿المائدة﴾

Those who believe and perform righteous deeds will incur no sin for
what they may have consumed (in the past), so long as they are mindful of God, believe and perform righteous deeds, then are mindful and
believe, then are mindful and virtuous. For God loves the virtuous (96)

Al-Mā'idah (The Feast) 5:96

جَعَلَ اللَّهُ الْكَعْبَةَ الْبَيْتَ الْحَرَامَ قِيَامًا لِلنَّاسِ وَالشَّهْرَ الْحَرَامَ وَالْهَدْيَ وَالْقَلَائِدَ ۚ ذَٰلِكَ لِتَعْلَمُوا أَنَّ اللَّهَ يَعْلَمُ مَا فِي السَّمَاوَاتِ وَمَا فِي الْأَرْضِ وَأَنَّ اللَّهَ بِكُلِّ شَيْءٍ عَلِيمٌ ﴿٩٧﴾ ﴿المائدة﴾

God made the *Ka'bah*, the Sacred House, a sanctuary for mankind, and the Sacred Months and the offerings (of animals) and the garlands. That you may be aware that God knows of all that is in the heavens and all that is on the earth, and that God is Knower of all things (97)

Al-Mā'idah (The Feast) 5:97

قُلْ لَا يَسْتَوِي الْخَبِيثُ وَالطَّيِّبُ وَلَوْ أَعْجَبَكَ كَثْرَةُ الْخَبِيثِ ، فَاتَّقُوا اللَّهَ يَا

أُولِي الْأَلْبَابِ لَعَلَّكُمْ تُفْلِحُونَ ﴿١٠٠﴾ ﴿المائدة﴾

Say, "The bad and the good are not equal, though you may be dazzled by the abundance of the bad." So be mindful of God, O possessors of intellect, so that you may prosper (100)

Al-Mā'idah (The Feast) 5:100

يَا أَيُّهَا الَّذِينَ آمَنُوا لَا تَسْأَلُوا عَنْ أَشْيَاءَ إِنْ تُبْدَ لَكُمْ تَسُؤْكُمْ وَإِنْ تَسْأَلُوا
عَنْهَا حِينَ يُنَزَّلُ الْقُرْآنُ تُبْدَ لَكُمْ عَفَا اللَّهُ عَنْهَاۗ واللَّهُ غَفُورٌ حَلِيمٌ ﴿١٠١﴾
﴿المائدة﴾

O you who believe! Do not ask about matters which if made known to you, might trouble you. If you ask about them while the Qur'an is being revealed, they will be made known to you. God has pardoned (you of) this and God is Forgiving, Forbearing (101)

Al-Mā'idah (The Feast) 5:101

قُل لِّمَن مَّا فِي السَّمَاوَاتِ وَالْأَرْضِ ۖ قُل لِّلَّهِ ۚ كَتَبَ عَلَىٰ نَفْسِهِ الرَّحْمَةَ ۚ
لَيَجْمَعَنَّكُمْ إِلَىٰ يَوْمِ الْقِيَامَةِ لَا رَيْبَ فِيهِ ۚ الَّذِينَ خَسِرُوا أَنفُسَهُمْ فَهُمْ لَا
يُؤْمِنُونَ ﴿١٢﴾ ﴿الأنعام﴾

Say, "Unto whom belongs all that is in the heavens and on the earth?"
Say, "Unto God. He has willed upon Himself (the law of) mercy. He
will surely gather you on the Day of Resurrection, which is beyond all
doubt. Those who have lost their souls will not believe" (12)

Al-Anām (Cattle) 6:12

وَلَهُ مَا سَكَنَ فِي اللَّيْلِ وَالنَّهَارِ ۚ وَهُوَ السَّمِيعُ الْعَلِيمُ ﴿١٣﴾ ﴿الأنعام﴾

"And His is all that dwells in the night and in the day. He is the All-Hearing, the All-Knowing" (13)

Al-Anām (Cattle) 6:13

وَإِذَا جَاءَكَ الَّذِينَ يُؤْمِنُونَ بِآيَاتِنَا فَقُلْ سَلَامٌ عَلَيْكُمْ ۖ كَتَبَ رَبُّكُمْ عَلَىٰ نَفْسِهِ
الرَّحْمَةَ ۖ أَنَّهُ مَنْ عَمِلَ مِنْكُمْ سُوءًا بِجَهَالَةٍ ثُمَّ تَابَ مِنْ بَعْدِهِ وَأَصْلَحَ فَأَنَّهُ
غَفُورٌ رَحِيمٌ ﴿٥٤﴾ ﴿الأنعام﴾

And when those who believe in our revelations come to thee, say, "Peace be upon you. Your Lord has willed upon Himself (the law of) mercy, that whoever among you does evil in ignorance and thereafter repents and corrects (himself), He is truly Forgiving, Merciful" (54)

Al-Anām (Cattle) 6:54

وَعِنْدَهُ مَفَاتِحُ الْغَيْبِ لَا يَعْلَمُهَا إِلَّا هُوَ ۚ وَيَعْلَمُ مَا فِي الْبَرِّ وَالْبَحْرِ ۚ وَمَا

تَسْقُطُ مِنْ وَرَقَةٍ إِلَّا يَعْلَمُهَا وَلَا حَبَّةٍ فِي ظُلُمَاتِ الْأَرْضِ وَلَا رَطْبٍ وَلَا يَابِسٍ

إِلَّا فِي كِتَابٍ مُبِينٍ ﴿٥٩﴾ ﴿الأنعام﴾

With Him are the keys of the Unseen, none knows them but He; and He knows all that is on the land and the sea. Not a leaf falls but with His knowledge, and not a grain in the darkness of the earth, nor anything fresh or dry (green or withered), but is recorded in a clear Book (59)

Al-Anām (Cattle) 6:59

ذَٰلِكُمُ اللَّهُ رَبُّكُمْ ۖ لَا إِلَٰهَ إِلَّا هُوَ ۖ خَالِقُ كُلِّ شَيْءٍ فَاعْبُدُوهُ ۚ وَهُوَ عَلَىٰ كُلِّ

شَيْءٍ وَكِيلٌ ﴿١٠٢﴾ ﴿الأنعام﴾

This is God, your Lord, there is no god but Him, the Creator of all things, so worship Him and He is Guardian of all things (102)

Al-Anām (Cattle) 6:102

لَا تُدْرِكُهُ الْأَبْصَارُ وَهُوَ يُدْرِكُ الْأَبْصَارَ ـ وَهُوَ اللَّطِيفُ الْخَبِيرُ ﴿١٠٣﴾

﴿الأنعام﴾

No vision can encompass Him, but He encompasses all vision and He is the Subtle, the All-Aware (103)

Al-Anām (Cattle) 6:103

قَدْ جَاءَكُمْ بَصَائِرُ مِنْ رَبِّكُمْ ۖ فَمَنْ أَبْصَرَ فَلِنَفْسِهِ ۖ وَمَنْ عَمِيَ فَعَلَيْهَا ۚ وَمَا أَنَا عَلَيْكُمْ بِحَفِيظٍ ﴿١٠٤﴾ ﴿الأنعام﴾

Insight has now come to you from your Lord; whoever sees it, it is for his own benefit; and whoever is blind, then it will be to his own hurt. And I am not a keeper over you (104)

Al-Anām (Cattle) 6:104

وَلَا تَقْرَبُوا مَالَ الْيَتِيمِ إِلَّا بِالَّتِي هِيَ أَحْسَنُ حَتَّىٰ يَبْلُغَ أَشُدَّهُۥ وَأَوْفُوا الْكَيْلَ

وَالْمِيزَانَ بِالْقِسْطِ ۖ لَا نُكَلِّفُ نَفْسًا إِلَّا وُسْعَهَا ۖ وَإِذَا قُلْتُمْ فَاعْدِلُوا وَلَوْ كَانَ

ذَا قُرْبَىٰ ۖ وَبِعَهْدِ اللَّهِ أَوْفُوا ۚ ذَٰلِكُمْ وَصَّاكُم بِهِ لَعَلَّكُمْ تَذَكَّرُونَ ﴿١٥٢﴾

﴿الأنعام﴾

And approach not the property of orphans, save with that which is better, till he reaches maturity. And give full measure and weight in justice. We burden no soul beyond what it can bear. And when you speak, be just, even if it be (against) a kinsman and fulfil your oath with God. This He has commanded upon you, so that you may remember (152)

Al-Anām (Cattle) 6:152

مَنْ جَاءَ بِالْحَسَنَةِ فَلَهُ عَشْرُ أَمْثَالِهَا۔وَمَنْ جَاءَ بِالسَّيِّئَةِ فَلَا يُجْزَىٰ إِلَّا مِثْلَهَا

وَهُمْ لَا يُظْلَمُونَ ﴿١٦٠﴾ ﴿الأنعام﴾

Whoever brings a good deed shall receive tenfold the like thereof;
but whoever brings an evil deed shall only be requited with the like
thereof; and they shall not be wronged (160)

Al-Anām (Cattle) 6:160

قُلْ إِنَّنِي هَدَانِي رَبِّي إِلَى صِرَاطٍ مُسْتَقِيمٍ دِينًا قِيَمًا مِلَّةَ إِبْرَاهِيمَ حَنِيفًا وَمَا كَانَ مِنَ الْمُشْرِكِينَ ﴿١٦١﴾ ﴿الأنعام﴾

Say "Truly my Lord has guided me unto a straight path, an upright religion, the faith of Abraham, a *hanīf* (a man of pure faith), and he was not of the idolaters" (161)

Al-Anām (Cattle) 6:161

قُل إِنَّ صَلَاتِي وَنُسُكِي وَمَحْيَايَ وَمَمَاتِي لِلَّهِ رَبِّ الْعَالَمِين ﴿١٦٢﴾
﴿الأنعام﴾

Say "Truly my prayer, and my rituals, and my living and my dying are
(all) for God, Lord of the Worlds" (162)

Al-Anām (Cattle) 6:162

قُلْ أَغَيْرَ اللَّهِ أَبْغِي رَبًّا وَهُوَ رَبُّ كُلِّ شَيْءٍ ۚ وَلَا تَكْسِبُ كُلُّ نَفْسٍ إِلَّا عَلَيْهَا ۚ
وَلَا تَزِرُ وَازِرَةٌ وِزْرَ أُخْرَىٰ ۚ ثُمَّ إِلَىٰ رَبِّكُمْ مَرْجِعُكُمْ فَيُنَبِّئُكُمْ بِمَا كُنْتُمْ فِيهِ
تَخْتَلِفُونَ ﴿١٦٤﴾ ﴿الأنعام﴾

Say "Shall I seek a Lord other than God, when He is the Lord of all things? Each soul earns only its own account, and none shall bear the burden of another. Then in the end unto your Lord is your return, and He will inform you about where you differed" (164)

Al-Anām (Cattle) 6:164

وَالَّذِينَ آمَنُوا وَعَمِلُوا الصَّالِحَاتِ لَا نُكَلِّفُ نَفْسًا إِلَّا وُسْعَهَا أُولَٰئِكَ أَصْحَابُ الْجَنَّةِ هُمْ فِيهَا خَالِدُونَ ﴿٤٢﴾ وَنَزَعْنَا مَا فِي صُدُورِهِمْ مِنْ غِلٍّ تَجْرِي مِنْ تَحْتِهِمُ الْأَنْهَارُ وَقَالُوا الْحَمْدُ لِلَّهِ الَّذِي هَدَانَا لِهَٰذَا وَمَا كُنَّا لِنَهْتَدِيَ لَوْلَا أَنْ هَدَانَا اللَّهُ لَقَدْ جَاءَتْ رُسُلُ رَبِّنَا بِالْحَقِّ وَنُودُوا أَنْ تِلْكُمُ الْجَنَّةُ أُورِثْتُمُوهَا بِمَا كُنْتُمْ تَعْمَلُونَ ﴿٤٣﴾ ﴿الأعراف﴾

But those who believe and perform righteous deeds - We burden no soul beyond what it can bear; it is they who are the inhabitants of paradise and therein they shall abide (42) And we shall remove whatever ill feelings within their hearts. Rivers flow beneath them, and they will say "Praise be to God, Who guided us unto this. We would not have been rightly guided, had God not guided us. The messengers of our Lord certainly came with the truth." And a voice will call out unto them "This is paradise, you have inherited it for what you used to do" (43)

Al-Arāf (The Elevations) 7:42-43

وَلَقَدْ جِئْنَاهُم بِكِتَابٍ فَصَّلْنَاهُ عَلَىٰ عِلْمٍ هُدًى وَرَحْمَةً لِقَوْمٍ يُؤْمِنُونَ ﴿٥٢﴾ ﴿الأعراف﴾

Indeed, We have brought unto them a Scripture, which We explained with knowledge, a guidance and a mercy for a people who believe (52)

Al-Arāf (The Elevations) 7:52

إِنَّ رَبَّكُمُ اللَّهُ الَّذِي خَلَقَ السَّمَاوَاتِ وَالْأَرْضَ فِي سِتَّةِ أَيَّامٍ ثُمَّ اسْتَوَىٰ
عَلَى الْعَرْشِ يُغْشِي اللَّيْلَ النَّهَارَ يَطْلُبُهُ حَثِيثًا وَالشَّمْسَ وَالْقَمَرَ وَالنُّجُومَ
مُسَخَّرَاتٍ بِأَمْرِهِ ۗ أَلَا لَهُ الْخَلْقُ وَالْأَمْرُ ۗ تَبَارَكَ اللَّهُ رَبُّ الْعَالَمِينَ ﴿٥٤﴾
﴿الأعراف﴾

Truly your Lord is God, Who created the heavens and the earth in six
Days, then mounted the Throne. He covers the night with the day, in
swift pursuit; and the sun and the moon and the stars are made subservient by His Command. His is all creation and command. Blessed is
God, Lord of the Worlds! (54)

Al-Araf (The Elevations) 7:54

ادْعُوا رَبَّكُمْ تَضَرُّعًا وَخُفْيَةً ۚ إِنَّهُ لَا يُحِبُّ الْمُعْتَدِينَ ﴿٥٥﴾ ﴿الأعراف﴾

Call upon your Lord humbly and privately. Truly He loves not the aggressors (55)

Al-Arāf (The Elevations) 7:55

وَلَا تُفْسِدُوا فِي الْأَرْضِ بَعْدَ إِصْلَاحِهَا وَادْعُوهُ خَوْفًا وَطَمَعًا ۚ إِنَّ رَحْمَتَ اللَّهِ
قَرِيبٌ مِنَ الْمُحْسِنِينَ ﴿٥٦﴾ ﴿الأعراف﴾

And do not spread corruption on earth, after it has been set in order,
and call upon Him in fear and in longing, truly the mercy of God is ever
near unto the virtuous (56)

Al-Arāf (The Elevations) 7:56

وَالَّذِينَ يُمَسِّكُونَ بِالكِتَابِ وَأَقَامُوا الصَّلَاةَ إِنَّا لَا نُضِيعُ أَجْرَ المُصلِحِينَ

﴿١٧٠﴾ ﴿الأعراف﴾

As for those who hold fast to the Scripture and are steadfast in prayer, truly We shall not deny the reward of the righteous (170)

Al-Arāf (The Elevations) 7:170

وَاذْكُر رَّبَّكَ فِي نَفْسِكَ تَضَرُّعًا وَخِيفَةً وَدُونَ الْجَهْرِ مِنَ الْقَوْلِ بِالْغُدُوِّ
وَالْآصَالِ وَلَا تَكُنْ مِنَ الْغَافِلِينَ ﴿٢٠٥﴾ إِنَّ الَّذِينَ عِنْدَ رَبِّكَ لَا يَسْتَكْبِرُونَ
عَنْ عِبَادَتِهِ وَيُسَبِّحُونَهُ وَلَهُ يَسْجُدُونَ ۩ ﴿٢٠٦﴾ ﴿الأعراف﴾

And remember thy Lord within yourself, humbly and with awe, and without being loud at morning and evening. And be not among the heedless (205) Truly those who are with thy Lord are not too proud to worship Him. And they glorify Him and prostate before Him (206)

Al-Arāf (The Elevations) 7:205-206

إِنَّمَا الْمُؤْمِنُونَ الَّذِينَ إِذَا ذُكِرَ اللَّهُ وَجِلَتْ قُلُوبُهُمْ وَإِذَا تُلِيَتْ عَلَيْهِمْ آيَاتُهُ زَادَتْهُمْ إِيمَانًا وَعَلَىٰ رَبِّهِمْ يَتَوَكَّلُونَ ﴿٢﴾ الَّذِينَ يُقِيمُونَ الصَّلَاةَ وَمِمَّا رَزَقْنَاهُمْ يُنْفِقُونَ ﴿٣﴾ أُولَٰئِكَ هُمُ الْمُؤْمِنُونَ حَقًّا ۚ لَهُمْ دَرَجَاتٌ عِنْدَ رَبِّهِمْ وَمَغْفِرَةٌ وَرِزْقٌ كَرِيمٌ ﴿٤﴾ ﴿الأنفال﴾

The believers are those who when God is mentioned their hearts tremble, and when His verses are recited unto them they increase their faith, and trust in their Lord (2) Those who are steadfast in prayer and spend from that which We have provided them (3) It is they who are truly believers. They have high rankings with their Lord, and forgiveness and a generous provision (4)

Al-Anfāl (The Spoils) 8:2-4

إِذْ تَسْتَغِيثُونَ رَبَّكُمْ فَاسْتَجَابَ لَكُمْ أَنِّي مُمِدُّكُم بِأَلْفٍ مِنَ الْمَلَائِكَةِ مُرْدِفِينَ ﴿٩﴾ وَمَا جَعَلَهُ اللَّهُ إِلَّا بُشْرَىٰ وَلِتَطْمَئِنَّ بِهِ قُلُوبُكُمْ ۚ وَمَا النَّصْرُ إِلَّا مِنْ عِندِ اللَّهِ ۚ إِنَّ اللَّهَ عَزِيزٌ حَكِيمٌ ﴿١٠﴾ ﴿الأنفال﴾

When you sought help of your Lord He responded to you "I shall aid you with a thousand angels rank upon rank" (9) And God ordained this only as a glad tiding, and that your hearts may be at peace. Indeed victory comes from God alone, Truly God is Almighty, Wise (10)

Al-Anfāl (The Spoils) 8:9-10

يَا أَيُّهَا الَّذِينَ آمَنُوا اسْتَجِيبُوا لِلَّهِ وَلِلرَّسُولِ إِذَا دَعَاكُمْ لِمَا يُحْيِيكُمْ وَاعْلَمُوا أَنَّ اللَّهَ يَحُولُ بَيْنَ الْمَرْءِ وَقَلْبِهِ وَأَنَّهُ إِلَيْهِ تُحْشَرُونَ ﴿٢٤﴾ ﴿الأنفال﴾

O you who believe! Respond to God and the Messenger when he calls you to that which gives you life. And know that God comes between a man and his heart, and that unto Him you shall be gathered (24)

Al-Anfāl (The Spoils) 8:24

وَاتَّقُوا فِتْنَةً لَا تُصِيبَنَّ الَّذِينَ ظَلَمُوا مِنْكُمْ خَاصَّةً ـوَاعْلَمُوا أَنَّ اللَّهَ شَدِيدُ الْعِقَابِ ﴿٢٥﴾ ﴿الأنفال﴾

And be mindful of a trial that will befall not only the wrong doers among you in particular; and know that God is severe in punishment (25)

Al-Anfāl (The Spoils) 8:25

وَاعْلَمُوا أَنَّمَا أَمْوَالُكُمْ وَأَوْلَادُكُمْ فِتْنَةٌ وَأَنَّ اللَّهَ عِنْدَهُ أَجْرٌ عَظِيمٌ ﴿٢٨﴾

﴿الأنفال﴾

And know that your wealth and your children are a trial and that with God is a tremendous reward (28)

Al-Anfāl (The Spoils) 8:28

يَا أَيُّهَا الَّذِينَ آمَنُوا إِنْ تَتَّقُوا اللَّهَ يَجْعَلْ لَكُمْ فُرْقَانًا وَيُكَفِّرْ عَنْكُمْ سَيِّئَاتِكُمْ وَيَغْفِرْ لَكُمْ ۚ وَاللَّهُ ذُو الْفَضْلِ الْعَظِيمِ ﴿٢٩﴾ ﴿الأنفال﴾

O you who believe! If you are mindful of God, He will grant you (a means of) discrimination (between right and wrong), and absolve you of your evil deeds, and forgive you; and God is of Infinite Bounty (29)

Al-Anfāl (The Spoils) 8:29

ذَٰلِكَ بِأَنَّ اللَّهَ لَمْ يَكُ مُغَيِّرًا نِعْمَةً أَنْعَمَهَا عَلَىٰ قَوْمٍ حَتَّىٰ يُغَيِّرُوا مَا بِأَنْفُسِهِمْ ٧ وَأَنَّ اللَّهَ سَمِيعٌ عَلِيمٌ ﴿٥٣﴾ ﴿الأنفال﴾

That is because God never changes a grace He has bestowed on a people until they first change what is within themselves. God is Hearing, Knowing (53)

Al-Anfāl (The Spoils) 8:53

الْمُنَافِقُونَ وَالْمُنَافِقَاتُ بَعْضُهُم مِنْ بَعْضٍ ۚ يَأْمُرُونَ بِالْمُنْكَرِ وَيَنْهَوْنَ عَنِ الْمَعْرُوفِ وَيَقْبِضُونَ أَيْدِيَهُمْ ۚ نَسُوا اللَّهَ فَنَسِيَهُمْ ۗ إِنَّ الْمُنَافِقِينَ هُمُ الْفَاسِقُونَ ﴿٦٧﴾ وَعَدَ اللَّهُ الْمُنَافِقِينَ وَالْمُنَافِقَاتِ وَالْكُفَّارَ نَارَ جَهَنَّمَ خَالِدِينَ فِيهَا ۚ هِيَ حَسْبُهُمْ ۚ وَلَعَنَهُمُ اللَّهُ ۖ وَلَهُمْ عَذَابٌ مُقِيمٌ ﴿٦٨﴾ ﴿التوبة﴾

The hypocrites, both men and women, are all of a kind. They instruct the wrong and forbid the right, and withhold their hands (from doing good). They forgot God, so He forgot them. Truly the hypocrites are iniquitous (67) God promised the hypocrites, both men and women, and the disbelievers the Fire of Hell, to abide therein. It shall suffice them. God has rejected them and theirs shall be lasting punishment (68)

Al-Tawbah (Repentance) 9:67-68

وَالْمُؤْمِنُونَ وَالْمُؤْمِنَاتُ بَعْضُهُمْ أَوْلِيَاءُ بَعْضٍ ۚ يَأْمُرُونَ بِالْمَعْرُوفِ وَيَنْهَوْنَ

عَنِ الْمُنْكَرِ وَيُقِيمُونَ الصَّلَاةَ وَيُؤْتُونَ الزَّكَاةَ وَيُطِيعُونَ اللَّهَ وَرَسُولَهُ ۚ أُولَٰئِكَ

سَيَرْحَمُهُمُ اللَّهُ ۗ إِنَّ اللَّهَ عَزِيزٌ حَكِيمٌ ﴿٧١﴾ ﴿التوبة﴾

And the believers, both men and women, are protectors of one another. They instruct the right and forbid the wrong, are steadfast in prayer, give the alms and obey God and His Messenger. They are the ones upon whom God will have mercy. Truly God is Almighty, Wise (71)

Al-Tawbah (Repentance) 9:71

154

وَعَدَ اللَّهُ الْمُؤْمِنِينَ وَالْمُؤْمِنَاتِ جَنَّاتٍ تَجْرِي مِنْ تَحْتِهَا الْأَنْهَارُ خَالِدِينَ فِيهَا وَمَسَاكِنَ طَيِّبَةً فِي جَنَّاتِ عَدْنٍ ۚ وَرِضْوَانٌ مِنَ اللَّهِ أَكْبَرُ ۚ ذَٰلِكَ هُوَ الْفَوْزُ الْعَظِيمُ ﴿٧٢﴾ ﴿التوبة﴾

God promised the believers, both men and women Gardens beneath which rivers flow abiding therein and goodly dwellings in Gardens of Eden. But contentment from God is greater, that is the supreme triumph (72)

Al-Tawbah (Repentance) 9:72

وَمِنَ الْأَعْرَابِ مَنْ يُؤْمِنُ بِاللَّهِ وَالْيَوْمِ الْآخِرِ وَيَتَّخِذُ مَا يُنْفِقُ قُرُبَاتٍ عِنْدَ اللَّهِ وَصَلَوَاتِ الرَّسُولِ ۚ أَلَا إِنَّهَا قُرْبَةٌ لَهُمْ ۚ سَيُدْخِلُهُمُ اللَّهُ فِي رَحْمَتِهِ ۚ إِنَّ اللَّهَ غَفُورٌ رَحِيمٌ ﴿٩٩﴾ ﴿التوبة﴾

And among the desert Arabs are those who believe in God and the Last Day, and regard what they spend as bringing them nearer to God and the prayers of the Messenger. Behold! It shall bring them nearer. God will admit them into His Mercy. Truly God is Forgiving, Merciful (99)

Al-Tawbah (Repentance) 9:99

وَالسَّابِقُونَ الْأَوَّلُونَ مِنَ الْمُهَاجِرِينَ وَالْأَنْصَارِ وَالَّذِينَ اتَّبَعُوهُمْ بِإِحْسَانٍ رَضِيَ اللَّهُ عَنْهُمْ وَرَضُوا عَنْهُ وَأَعَدَّ لَهُمْ جَنَّاتٍ تَجْرِي تَحْتَهَا الْأَنْهَارُ خَالِدِينَ فِيهَا أَبَدًا ۚ ذَٰلِكَ الْفَوْزُ الْعَظِيمُ ﴿١٠٠﴾ ﴿التوبة﴾

And as for the foremost first among the emigrants and the helpers and those who followed them in virtue, God is content with them and they content with Him, and He promised them Gardens beneath which rivers flow abiding therein forever. That is the supreme triumph (100)

Al-Tawbah (Repentance) 9:100

أَلَمْ يَعْلَمُوا أَنَّ اللَّهَ هُوَ يَقْبَلُ التَّوْبَةَ عَنْ عِبَادِهِ وَيَأْخُذُ الصَّدَقَاتِ وَأَنَّ اللَّهَ

هُوَ التَّوَّابُ الرَّحِيمُ ﴿١٠٤﴾ ﴿التوبة﴾

Do they not know that God Himself accepts repentance from His servants, and receives the alms, and that God is the Relenting, the Merciful (104)

Al-Tawbah (Repentance) 9:104

يَا أَيُّهَا الَّذِينَ آمَنُوا اتَّقُوا اللَّهَ وَكُونُوا مَعَ الصَّادِقِينَ ﴿١١٩﴾ ﴿التوبة﴾

O you who believe! Be mindful of God and be among the truthful (119)

Al-Tawbah (Repentance) 9:119

إِنَّ رَبَّكُمُ اللَّهُ الَّذِي خَلَقَ السَّمَاوَاتِ وَالْأَرْضَ فِي سِتَّةِ أَيَّامٍ ثُمَّ اسْتَوَىٰ عَلَى الْعَرْشِ يُدَبِّرُ الْأَمْرَ مَا مِنْ شَفِيعٍ إِلَّا مِنْ بَعْدِ إِذْنِهِ ذَلِكُمُ اللَّهُ رَبُّكُمْ فَاعْبُدُوهُ أَفَلَا تَذَكَّرُونَ ﴿٣﴾ ﴿يونس﴾

Truly your Lord is God, Who created the heavens and the earth in six Days, then mounted the Throne, governing everything. There is none that could intercede with Him, save by His Leave. That is God, your Lord; so worship Him. Will you not remember? (3)

Yūnus (Jonah) 10:3

إِلَيْهِ مَرْجِعُكُمْ جَمِيعًا ۚ وَعْدَ اللَّهِ حَقًّا ۚ إِنَّهُ يَبْدَأُ الْخَلْقَ ثُمَّ يُعِيدُهُ لِيَجْزِيَ الَّذِينَ آمَنُوا وَعَمِلُوا الصَّالِحَاتِ بِالْقِسْطِ ۚ وَالَّذِينَ كَفَرُوا لَهُمْ شَرَابٌ مِنْ حَمِيمٍ وَعَذَابٌ أَلِيمٌ بِمَا كَانُوا يَكْفُرُونَ ﴿٤﴾ ﴿يونس﴾

Unto Him you shall all return. God's promise is true. Verily He begins creation then brings it forth anew to reward those who believe and perform righteous deeds justly. And those who disbelieve theirs shall be a drink of boiling liquid and an agonizing torment for having disbelieved (4)

Yūnus (Jonah) 10:4

هُوَ الَّذِي جَعَلَ الشَّمْسَ ضِيَاءً وَالْقَمَرَ نُورًا وَقَدَّرَهُ مَنَازِلَ لِتَعْلَمُوا عَدَدَ
السِّنِينَ وَالْحِسَابَ ، مَا خَلَقَ اللَّهُ ذَٰلِكَ إِلَّا بِالْحَقِّ ، يُفَصِّلُ الْآيَاتِ لِقَوْمٍ
يَعْلَمُونَ ﴿٥﴾ ﴿يونس﴾

It is He Who made the sun a radiance, and the moon a light, and deter-
mined for it phases so that you might know the number of years and
how to calculate time. God did not create these save with truth. He
detailed the revelations for a people who understand (5)

Yūnus (Jonah) 10:5

إِنَّ فِي اخْتِلَافِ اللَّيْلِ وَالنَّهَارِ وَمَا خَلَقَ اللَّهُ فِي السَّمَاوَاتِ وَالْأَرْضِ لَآيَاتٍ لِقَوْمٍ يَتَّقُونَ ﴿٦﴾ ﴿يونس﴾

Truly in the variation of the night and the day and in all that God created in the heavens and the earth are signs for a people who are mindful of Him (6)

Yūnus (Jonah) 10:6

إِنَّ الَّذِينَ آمَنُوا وَعَمِلُوا الصَّالِحَاتِ يَهْدِيهِمْ رَبُّهُمْ بِإِيمَانِهِمْ تَجْرِي مِنْ تَحْتِهِمُ الْأَنْهَارُ فِي جَنَّاتِ النَّعِيمِ ﴿٩﴾ دَعْوَاهُمْ فِيهَا سُبْحَانَكَ اللَّهُمَّ وَتَحِيَّتُهُمْ فِيهَا سَلَامٌ وَآخِرُ دَعْوَاهُمْ أَنِ الْحَمْدُ لِلَّهِ رَبِّ الْعَالَمِينَ ﴿١٠﴾ ﴿يونس﴾

Truly those who believe and perform righteous deeds, their Lord guides them by their faith. Rivers flow beneath them in Gardens of bliss (9) Their prayer therein shall be, "Glory be to Thee, O God!" and their greeting therein shall be "Peace." And the last (part) of their prayer shall be, "Praise be to God, Lord of the Worlds" (10)

Yūnus (Jonah) 10:9-10

وَاللَّهُ يَدْعُوا إِلَى دَارِ السَّلَامِ وَيَهْدِي مَنْ يَشَاءُ إِلَى صِرَاطٍ مُسْتَقِيمٍ ﴿٢٥﴾

﴿يونس﴾

And God calls unto the Abode of Peace, and guides whom He will unto a straight path (25)

Yūnus (Jonah) 10:25

لِلَّذِينَ أَحْسَنُوا الْحُسْنَىٰ وَزِيَادَةٌ ۖ وَلَا يَرْهَقُ وُجُوهَهُمْ قَتَرٌ وَلَا ذِلَّةٌ ۚ أُولَـٰئِكَ أَصْحَابُ الْجَنَّةِ ۖ هُمْ فِيهَا خَالِدُونَ ﴿٢٦﴾ ﴿يونس﴾

For those who do good shall be the best reward and more besides. Neither darkness nor shame shall come near their faces. It is they who are inhabitants of paradise; therein they shall abide (26)

Yūnus (Jonah) 10:26

قُلْ مَنْ يَرْزُقُكُمْ مِنَ السَّمَاءِ وَالْأَرْضِ أَمَّنْ يَمْلِكُ السَّمْعَ وَالْأَبْصَارَ وَمَنْ يُخْرِجُ
الْحَيَّ مِنَ الْمَيِّتِ وَيُخْرِجُ الْمَيِّتَ مِنَ الْحَيِّ وَمَنْ يُدَبِّرُ الْأَمْرَ ۚ فَسَيَقُولُونَ
اللَّهُ ۚ فَقُلْ أَفَلَا تَتَّقُونَ ﴿٣١﴾ ﴿يونس﴾

Say "Who provides for you from the heaven and the earth? Or who has power over hearing and sight? And who brings forth the living from the dead and brings forth the dead from the living? And who governs everything?" They will say "God." Then say, "Will you not then be conscious of Him?" (31)

Yūnus (Jonah) 10:31

وَمَا كَانَ هَٰذَا الْقُرْآنُ أَنْ يُفْتَرَىٰ مِنْ دُونِ اللَّهِ وَلَٰكِنْ تَصْدِيقَ الَّذِي بَيْنَ يَدَيْهِ وَتَفْصِيلَ الْكِتَابِ لَا رَيْبَ فِيهِ مِنْ رَبِّ الْعَالَمِينَ ﴿٣٧﴾ أَمْ يَقُولُونَ افْتَرَاهُ قُلْ فَأْتُوا بِسُورَةٍ مِثْلِهِ وَادْعُوا مَنِ اسْتَطَعْتُمْ مِنْ دُونِ اللَّهِ إِنْ كُنْتُمْ صَادِقِينَ ﴿٣٨﴾ ﴿يونس﴾

And this Qur'an could not have been produced by anyone other than God, rather it is a confirmation of that which was (revealed) before it and an explanation of the Scripture. There is no doubt—it is from the Lord of the Worlds (37) Or they say "He has invented it" Say, "Then bring a *surah* like it, and call upon whomever you can besides God, if you are truthful" (38)

Yūnus (Jonah) 10:37-38

أَلَا إِنَّ أَوْلِيَاءَ اللَّهِ لَا خَوْفٌ عَلَيْهِمْ وَلَا هُمْ يَحْزَنُونَ ﴿٦٢﴾ الَّذِينَ آمَنُوا وَكَانُوا يَتَّقُونَ ﴿٦٣﴾ لَهُمُ الْبُشْرَىٰ فِي الْحَيَاةِ الدُّنْيَا وَفِي الْآخِرَةِ ۚ لَا تَبْدِيلَ لِكَلِمَاتِ اللَّهِ ۚ ذَٰلِكَ هُوَ الْفَوْزُ الْعَظِيمُ ﴿٦٤﴾ وَلَا يَحْزُنْكَ قَوْلُهُمْ ۘ إِنَّ الْعِزَّةَ لِلَّهِ جَمِيعًا ۚ هُوَ السَّمِيعُ الْعَلِيمُ ﴿٦٥﴾ ﴿يونس﴾

Lo! Truly those who are close to God no fear shall come upon them, nor shall they grieve (62) Those who believe and were conscious of Him (63) Theirs are glad tidings in the life of this world and in the Hereafter, there is no altering the Words of God, that is the supreme triumph (64) And be not grieved by their sayings. Power belongs wholly to God, He is the All-Hearing, the All-Knowing (65)

Yūnus (Jonah) 10:62-65

الر ۚ كِتَابٌ أُحْكِمَتْ آيَاتُهُ ثُمَّ فُصِّلَتْ مِنْ لَدُنْ حَكِيمٍ خَبِيرٍ ﴿١﴾ ﴿هود﴾

Alif. Lām. Rā. (This is) a Scripture, whose verses are perfected and then clearly explained, from One who is All-Wise, All-Aware (1)

Hūd (Hud) 11:1

وَأَنِ اسْتَغْفِرُوا رَبَّكُمْ ثُمَّ تُوبُوا إِلَيْهِ يُمَتِّعْكُم مَّتَاعًا حَسَنًا إِلَى أَجَلٍ مُّسَمًّى

وَيُؤْتِ كُلَّ ذِي فَضْلٍ فَضْلَهُۥ وَإِن تَوَلَّوْا فَإِنِّي أَخَافُ عَلَيْكُمْ عَذَابَ يَوْمٍ

كَبِيرٍ ﴿٣﴾ إِلَى اللَّهِ مَرْجِعُكُمْ وَهُوَ عَلَىٰ كُلِّ شَيْءٍ قَدِيرٌ ﴿٤﴾ ﴿هود﴾

And ask forgiveness of your Lord and then repent to Him. He will grant you goodly enjoyment until a time appointed and will give His grace unto everyone who has merit. But if you turn away, I fear for you the retribution of a great Day (3) Unto God is your return, and He is Powerful over all things (4)

Hud (Hud) 11:3-4

وَاسْتَغْفِرُوا رَبَّكُمْ ثُمَّ تُوبُوا إِلَيْهِ ۚ إِنَّ رَبِّي رَحِيمٌ وَدُودٌ ﴿٩٠﴾ ﴿هود﴾

And ask forgiveness of your Lord and then repent to Him. Truly my Lord is Merciful, Most Loving (90)

Hūd (Hud) 11:90

وَلِلَّهِ غَيْبُ السَّمَاوَاتِ وَالْأَرْضِ وَإِلَيْهِ يُرْجَعُ الْأَمْرُ كُلُّهُ فَاعْبُدْهُ وَتَوَكَّلْ عَلَيْهِ ۚ

وَمَا رَبُّكَ بِغَافِلٍ عَمَّا تَعْمَلُونَ ﴿١٢٣﴾ ﴿هود﴾

Unto God belongs the Unseen in the heavens and the earth, and unto Him all matters return. So worship Him, and trust in Him and thy Lord is not unaware of all that you do (123)

Hūd (Hud) 11:123

وَكَذَلِكَ مَكَّنَّا لِيُوسُفَ فِي الْأَرْضِ يَتَبَوَّأُ مِنْهَا حَيْثُ يَشَاءُ ۚ نُصِيبُ بِرَحْمَتِنَا مَنْ نَشَاءُ ۖ وَلَا نُضِيعُ أَجْرَ الْمُحْسِنِينَ ﴿٥٦﴾ ﴿يوسف﴾

Thus We established Joseph in the land, to settle in it wherever he wished. We bestow Our mercy upon whomever We will and We do not fail the reward of the virtuous (56)

Yūsuf (Joseph) 12:56

وَلَأَجْرُ الْآخِرَةِ خَيْرٌ لِلَّذِينَ آمَنُوا وَكَانُوا يَتَّقُونَ ﴿٥٧﴾ ﴿يوسف﴾

And the reward of the Hereafter is better for those who believe and are mindful (of God) (57)

Yūsuf (Joseph) 12:57

قَالُوا أَإِنَّكَ لَأَنْتَ يُوسُفُ ـ قَالَ أَنَا يُوسُفُ وَهَٰذَا أَخِي ـ قَدْ مَنَّ اللَّهُ عَلَيْنَا ـ إِنَّهُ مَنْ يَتَّقِ وَيَصْبِرْ فَإِنَّ اللَّهَ لَا يُضِيعُ أَجْرَ الْمُحْسِنِينَ ﴿٩٠﴾ قَالُوا تَاللَّهِ لَقَدْ آثَرَكَ اللَّهُ عَلَيْنَا وَإِنْ كُنَّا لَخَاطِئِينَ ﴿٩١﴾ قَالَ لَا تَثْرِيبَ عَلَيْكُمُ الْيَوْمَ ـ يَغْفِرُ اللَّهُ لَكُمْ ـ وَهُوَ أَرْحَمُ الرَّاحِمِينَ ﴿٩٢﴾ ﴿يوسف﴾

They said, "Is it indeed thou who art Joseph?" He said, "I am Joseph and this is my brother. God has indeed been gracious to us. Verily, he who is mindful and patient; truly God does not fail the reward of the virtuous" (90) They said, "By God! Truly God has favoured thee over us, and certainly we were at fault" (91) He said "No blame (shall fall) upon you today. May God forgive you; He is the Most Merciful of the merciful" (92)

Yūsuf (Joseph) 12:90-92

رَبِّ قَد آتَيتَني مِنَ المُلكِ وَعَلَّمتَني مِن تَأويلِ الأَحاديثِ ، فاطِرَ السَّماواتِ وَالأَرضِ أَنتَ وَلِيّي فِي الدُّنيا وَالآخِرَةِ ، تَوَفَّني مُسلِمًا وَأَلحِقني بِالصّالِحينَ ﴿١٠١﴾ ﴿يوسف﴾

My Lord, you have bestowed upon me sovereignty and have taught me something of the interpretation of dreams. Creator of the heavens and the earth, you are my Guardian in this world and in the Hereafter. Let me die as one who submitted to Thy will and unite me with the righteous

Yūsuf (Joseph) 12:101

أَفَمَنْ يَعْلَمُ أَنَّمَا أُنْزِلَ إِلَيْكَ مِنْ رَبِّكَ الْحَقُّ كَمَنْ هُوَ أَعْمَىٰ ۚ إِنَّمَا يَتَذَكَّرُ

أُولُو الْأَلْبَابِ ﴿١٩﴾ الَّذِينَ يُوفُونَ بِعَهْدِ اللَّهِ وَلَا يَنْقُضُونَ الْمِيثَاقَ ﴿٢٠﴾

وَالَّذِينَ يَصِلُونَ مَا أَمَرَ اللَّهُ بِهِ أَنْ يُوصَلَ وَيَخْشَوْنَ رَبَّهُمْ وَيَخَافُونَ سُوءَ

الْحِسَابِ ﴿٢١﴾ وَالَّذِينَ صَبَرُوا ابْتِغَاءَ وَجْهِ رَبِّهِمْ وَأَقَامُوا الصَّلَاةَ وَأَنْفَقُوا

مِمَّا رَزَقْنَاهُمْ سِرًّا وَعَلَانِيَةً وَيَدْرَءُونَ بِالْحَسَنَةِ السَّيِّئَةَ أُولَٰئِكَ لَهُمْ عُقْبَى

الدَّارِ ﴿٢٢﴾ جَنَّاتُ عَدْنٍ يَدْخُلُونَهَا وَمَنْ صَلَحَ مِنْ آبَائِهِمْ وَأَزْوَاجِهِمْ

وَذُرِّيَّاتِهِمْ ۖ وَالْمَلَائِكَةُ يَدْخُلُونَ عَلَيْهِمْ مِنْ كُلِّ بَابٍ ﴿٢٣﴾ سَلَامٌ عَلَيْكُمْ بِمَا

صَبَرْتُمْ ۚ فَنِعْمَ عُقْبَى الدَّارِ ﴿٢٤﴾ ﴿الرعد﴾

Is he who knows that what is sent down to unto thee from thy Lord is the truth like one who is blind? Only those who possess intellect will remember (19) Those who fulfil the oath with God and do not break the covenant (20) Who join together what God commanded to be joined, and are in awe of their Lord and fear an awful reckoning (21) And who are patient, seeking their Lord's countenance, and steadfast in prayer, and spend from that which We have provided them, secretly and openly, and who repel evil with good. Theirs shall be the sequel of the (heavenly) Abode (22) Gardens of Eden, which they shall enter along with their righteous ancestors, their spouses, and their descendants; and the angels shall enter upon them from every gate (23) "Peace be upon you for your patience" How excellent is the final Abode (24)

Al-Ra'd (Thunder) 13:19-24

الَّذِينَ آمَنُوا وَتَطْمَئِنُّ قُلُوبُهُم بِذِكْرِ اللَّهِ ۗ أَلَا بِذِكْرِ اللَّهِ تَطْمَئِنُّ الْقُلُوبُ
﴿٢٨﴾ ﴿الرعد﴾

Those who believe and whose hearts are at peace in the remembrance of God. Truly in the remembrance of God are hearts at peace (28)

Al-Ra'd (Thunder) 13:28

الَّذِينَ آمَنُوا وَعَمِلُوا الصَّالِحَاتِ طُوبَىٰ لَهُمْ وَحُسْنُ مَآبٍ ﴿٢٩﴾ ﴿الرعد﴾

Those who believe and perform righteous deeds theirs is joyfulness and a beautiful return (29)

Al-Ra'd (Thunder) 13:29

الر ۚ كِتَابٌ أَنْزَلْنَاهُ إِلَيْكَ لِتُخْرِجَ النَّاسَ مِنَ الظُّلُمَاتِ إِلَى النُّورِ بِإِذْنِ رَبِّهِمْ إِلَىٰ صِرَاطِ الْعَزِيزِ الْحَمِيدِ ﴿١﴾ ﴿إبراهيم﴾

Alif. Lām. Rā. (This is) a Scripture which We have sent down unto thee (Muhammad), that thou might bring forth mankind out of the depths of darkness into the light, by the leave of their Lord, unto the path of the Almighty, the Praised (1)

Ibrāhim (Abraham) 14:1

وَإِذْ تَأَذَّنَ رَبُّكُمْ لَئِنْ شَكَرْتُمْ لَأَزِيدَنَّكُمْ ـ وَلَئِنْ كَفَرْتُمْ إِنَّ عَذَابِي لَشَدِيدٌ ﴿٧﴾ ﴿إبراهيم﴾

And when your Lord proclaimed "If you give thanks, I will give you more; but if you are ungrateful, truly My punishment is severe" (7)

Ibrāhim (Abraham) 14:7

وَمَا لَنَا أَلَّا نَتَوَكَّلَ عَلَى اللَّهِ وَقَدْ هَدَانَا سُبُلَنَا ۚ وَلَنَصْبِرَنَّ عَلَىٰ مَا آذَيْتُمُونَا ۚ

وَعَلَى اللَّهِ فَلْيَتَوَكَّلِ الْمُتَوَكِّلُونَ ﴿١٢﴾ ﴿إبراهيم﴾

"And why should we not trust in God, when He has guided us in our ways? And we shall surely endure patiently, whatever harm you do to us. And in God let them place their trust" (12)

Ibrāhim (Abraham) 14:12

قُل لِعِبَادِيَ الَّذِينَ آمَنُوا يُقِيمُوا الصَّلَاةَ وَيُنْفِقُوا مِمَّا رَزَقْنَاهُمْ سِرًّا وَعَلَانِيَةً مِنْ قَبْلِ أَنْ يَأْتِيَ يَوْمٌ لَا بَيْعٌ فِيهِ وَلَا خِلَالٌ ﴿٣١﴾ ﴿إبراهيم﴾

Tell My servants who believe to establish the prayers and spend from that which We have provided them, secretly and openly, before a Day comes where there shall be neither bargaining nor befriending (31)

Ibrāhim (Abraham) 14:31

وَآتَاكُم مِّن كُلِّ مَا سَأَلْتُمُوهُ ۚ وَإِن تَعُدُّوا نِعْمَتَ اللَّهِ لَا تُحْصُوهَا ۗ إِنَّ

الْإِنسَانَ لَظَلُومٌ كَفَّارٌ ﴿٣٤﴾ ﴿إبراهيم﴾

And He gives you of all you ask of Him, and if you were to count the
Blessings of God, you could never compute them. Truly mankind is
wrongdoing, ungrateful (34)

Ibrāhim (Abraham) 14:34

رَبِّ إِنَّهُنَّ أَضْلَلْنَ كَثِيرًا مِنَ النَّاسِ ۔ فَمَنْ تَبِعَنِي فَإِنَّهُ مِنِّي ۔ وَمَنْ عَصَانِي
فَإِنَّكَ غَفُورٌ رَحِيمٌ ﴿٣٦﴾ رَبَّنَا إِنِّي أَسْكَنْتُ مِنْ ذُرِّيَّتِي بِوَادٍ غَيْرِ ذِي زَرْعٍ
عِنْدَ بَيْتِكَ الْمُحَرَّمِ رَبَّنَا لِيُقِيمُوا الصَّلَاةَ فَاجْعَلْ أَفْئِدَةً مِنَ النَّاسِ تَهْوِي
إِلَيْهِمْ وَارْزُقْهُمْ مِنَ الثَّمَرَاتِ لَعَلَّهُمْ يَشْكُرُونَ ﴿٣٧﴾ ﴿إبراهيم﴾

"My Lord! They have surely led astray many among mankind. So whoever follows me truly he is of me. And whoever disobeys me, truly
Thou art Forgiving, Merciful (36) Our Lord! Verily I have settled some
of my offspring in a valley without cultivation by Thy Sacred House,
our Lord, so that they might establish the prayer. So cause the hearts of
men to yearn toward them, and provide them with fruits so that they
may be thankful" (37)

Ibrāhim (Abraham) 14:36-37

الْحَمْدُ لِلَّهِ الَّذِي وَهَبَ لِي عَلَى الْكِبَرِ إِسْمَاعِيلَ وَإِسْحَاقَ ، إِنَّ رَبِّي
لَسَمِيعُ الدُّعَاءِ ﴿٣٩﴾ رَبِّ اجْعَلْنِي مُقِيمَ الصَّلَاةِ وَمِنْ ذُرِّيَّتِي، رَبَّنَا وَتَقَبَّلْ
دُعَاءِ ﴿٤٠﴾ رَبَّنَا اغْفِرْ لِي وَلِوَالِدَيَّ وَلِلْمُؤْمِنِينَ يَوْمَ يَقُومُ الْحِسَابُ ﴿٤١﴾
﴿إبراهيم﴾

"Praise be to God, Who bestowed upon me in my old age Ishmael and Isaac. Truly my Lord is the Hearer of prayer (39) My Lord! Make me steadfast in prayer and my offspring. Our Lord! Accept my request (40) Our Lord! Forgive me and my parents and the believers on the Day when the Reckoning comes" (41)

Ibrāhim (Abraham) 14:39-41

وَمَا خَلَقْنَا السَّمَاوَاتِ وَالْأَرْضَ وَمَا بَيْنَهُمَا إِلَّا بِالْحَقِّ ۗ وَإِنَّ السَّاعَةَ لَآتِيَةٌ ۖ فَاصْفَحِ الصَّفْحَ الْجَمِيلَ ﴿٨٥﴾ ﴿الحجر﴾

We did not create the heavens and the earth and all that is between them save with truth. And truly the Hour is coming. So forbear with a gracious forbearance (85)

Al-Hijr (Hijr) 15:85

فَسَبِّح بِحَمدِ رَبِّكَ وَكُن مِنَ السَّاجِدينَ ﴿٩٨﴾ ﴿الحجر﴾

So glorify the praise of your Lord and be among those who prostrate themselves (before Him) (98)

Al-Hijr (Hijr) 15:98

وَإِنْ تَعُدُّوا نِعْمَةَ اللَّهِ لَا تُحْصُوهَا ۚ إِنَّ اللَّهَ لَغَفُورٌ رَحِيمٌ ﴿١٨﴾ ﴿النحل﴾

If you tried to count the Blessings of God, you could never compute them. Truly God is Forgiving, Merciful (18)

Al-Nahl (The Bee) 16:18

وَقِيلَ لِلَّذِينَ اتَّقَوْا مَاذَا أَنْزَلَ رَبُّكُمْ ۚ قَالُوا خَيْرًا ۚ لِلَّذِينَ أَحْسَنُوا فِي هَٰذِهِ
الدُّنْيَا حَسَنَةٌ ۚ وَلَدَارُ الْآخِرَةِ خَيْرٌ ۚ وَلَنِعْمَ دَارُ الْمُتَّقِينَ ﴿٣٠﴾ جَنَّاتُ عَدْنٍ
يَدْخُلُونَهَا تَجْرِي مِنْ تَحْتِهَا الْأَنْهَارُ ۖ لَهُمْ فِيهَا مَا يَشَاءُونَ ۚ كَذَٰلِكَ يَجْزِي
اللَّهُ الْمُتَّقِينَ ﴿٣١﴾ الَّذِينَ تَتَوَفَّاهُمُ الْمَلَائِكَةُ طَيِّبِينَ ۙ يَقُولُونَ سَلَامٌ عَلَيْكُمُ
ادْخُلُوا الْجَنَّةَ بِمَا كُنْتُمْ تَعْمَلُونَ ﴿٣٢﴾ ﴿النحل﴾

And when those who are conscious of God are asked "What has your Lord sent down?" They will say "Goodness." For those who do good in this world there shall be good and the abode of the Hereafter is better. Excellent indeed is the abode of the God-conscious (30) Gardens of Eden shall they enter beneath which rivers flow, wherein they shall have whatever they wish. Thus does God reward those who are conscious of Him (31) Those whose lives the angels take while they are in a state of goodness, they will say "Peace be upon you! Enter paradise by virtue of what you used to do" (32)

Al-Nahl (The Bee) 16:30-32

إِنَّمَا قَوْلُنَا لِشَيْءٍ إِذَا أَرَدْنَاهُ أَنْ نَقُولَ لَهُ كُنْ فَيَكُونُ ﴿٤٠﴾ وَالَّذِينَ هَاجَرُوا فِي اللَّهِ مِنْ بَعْدِ مَا ظُلِمُوا لَنُبَوِّئَنَّهُمْ فِي الدُّنْيَا حَسَنَةً وَلَأَجْرُ الْآخِرَةِ أَكْبَرُ لَوْ كَانُوا يَعْلَمُونَ ﴿٤١﴾ الَّذِينَ صَبَرُوا وَعَلَىٰ رَبِّهِمْ يَتَوَكَّلُونَ ﴿٤٢﴾ ﴿النحل﴾

Whenever We will anything to be, We but say to it "Be!" and it is (40) And those who emigrated in God's cause after being wronged, We shall certainly settle them in a good place in this world. But the reward of the Hereafter is far greater, if they but knew (41) They are the steadfast and put their trust in their Lord (42)

Al-Nahl (The Bee) 16:40-42

وَمَا أَنْزَلْنَا عَلَيْكَ الْكِتَابَ إِلَّا لِتُبَيِّنَ لَهُمُ الَّذِي اخْتَلَفُوا فِيهِ ۙ وَهُدًى وَرَحْمَةً

لِقَوْمٍ يُؤْمِنُونَ ﴿٦٤﴾ ﴿النحل﴾

And unto thee We have sent down the Scripture only so that you might
make clear unto them that where they differed, and a guidance and a
mercy for a people who believe (64)

Al-Nahl (The Bee) 16:64

وَاللَّهُ أَنْزَلَ مِنَ السَّمَاءِ مَاءً فَأَحْيَا بِهِ الْأَرْضَ بَعْدَ مَوْتِهَا ۚ إِنَّ فِي ذَٰلِكَ لَآيَةً لِقَوْمٍ يَسْمَعُونَ ﴿٦٥﴾ وَإِنَّ لَكُمْ فِي الْأَنْعَامِ لَعِبْرَةً ۖ نُسْقِيكُمْ مِمَّا فِي بُطُونِهِ مِنْ بَيْنِ فَرْثٍ وَدَمٍ لَبَنًا خَالِصًا سَائِغًا لِلشَّارِبِينَ ﴿٦٦﴾ وَمِنْ ثَمَرَاتِ النَّخِيلِ وَالْأَعْنَابِ تَتَّخِذُونَ مِنْهُ سَكَرًا وَرِزْقًا حَسَنًا ۗ إِنَّ فِي ذَٰلِكَ لَآيَةً لِقَوْمٍ يَعْقِلُونَ ﴿٦٧﴾ وَأَوْحَىٰ رَبُّكَ إِلَى النَّحْلِ أَنِ اتَّخِذِي مِنَ الْجِبَالِ بُيُوتًا وَمِنَ الشَّجَرِ وَمِمَّا يَعْرِشُونَ ﴿٦٨﴾ ثُمَّ كُلِي مِنْ كُلِّ الثَّمَرَاتِ فَاسْلُكِي سُبُلَ رَبِّكِ ذُلُلًا ۚ يَخْرُجُ مِنْ بُطُونِهَا شَرَابٌ مُخْتَلِفٌ أَلْوَانُهُ فِيهِ شِفَاءٌ لِلنَّاسِ ۗ إِنَّ فِي ذَٰلِكَ لَآيَةً لِقَوْمٍ يَتَفَكَّرُونَ ﴿٦٩﴾ ﴿النحل﴾

And God sent down water from the sky thereby reviving the earth after its death. Surely in this is a sign for a people who listen (65) And surely in the cattle (too) is a lesson for you, We give you to drink from the contents of their bellies, between excretions and blood, pure milk, pleasant to those who drink it (66) And from the fruit of the date-palms and grapes you take from it a sweet drink and wholesome provisions. Surely in this is a sign for a people who use their intellect (67) And thy Lord inspired the bee, "Take up from among the mountains habitats and in the trees and in what they (people) build (68) Then eat from all kinds of fruit, and follow the paths of your Lord made easy." From their bellies comes a drink of different colours of which there is healing for mankind. Surely in this is a sign for a people who reflect (69)

Al-Nahl (The Bee) 16:65-69

وَاللَّهُ أَخْرَجَكُمْ مِنْ بُطُونِ أُمَّهَاتِكُمْ لَا تَعْلَمُونَ شَيْئًا وَجَعَلَ لَكُمُ السَّمْعَ وَالْأَبْصَارَ وَالْأَفْئِدَةَ لَعَلَّكُمْ تَشْكُرُونَ ﴿٧٨﴾ أَلَمْ يَرَوْا إِلَى الطَّيْرِ مُسَخَّرَاتٍ فِي جَوِّ السَّمَاءِ مَا يُمْسِكُهُنَّ إِلَّا اللَّهُ ۗ إِنَّ فِي ذَٰلِكَ لَآيَاتٍ لِقَوْمٍ يُؤْمِنُونَ ﴿٧٩﴾ وَاللَّهُ جَعَلَ لَكُمْ مِنْ بُيُوتِكُمْ سَكَنًا وَجَعَلَ لَكُمْ مِنْ جُلُودِ الْأَنْعَامِ بُيُوتًا تَسْتَخِفُّونَهَا يَوْمَ ظَعْنِكُمْ وَيَوْمَ إِقَامَتِكُمْ ۙ وَمِنْ أَصْوَافِهَا وَأَوْبَارِهَا وَأَشْعَارِهَا أَثَاثًا وَمَتَاعًا إِلَىٰ حِينٍ ﴿٨٠﴾ وَاللَّهُ جَعَلَ لَكُمْ مِمَّا خَلَقَ ظِلَالًا وَجَعَلَ لَكُمْ مِنَ الْجِبَالِ أَكْنَانًا وَجَعَلَ لَكُمْ سَرَابِيلَ تَقِيكُمُ الْحَرَّ وَسَرَابِيلَ تَقِيكُمْ بَأْسَكُمْ ۚ كَذَٰلِكَ يُتِمُّ نِعْمَتَهُ عَلَيْكُمْ لَعَلَّكُمْ تُسْلِمُونَ ﴿٨١﴾ ﴿النحل﴾

And God brought you forth from the wombs of your mothers knowing nothing, and He gave you hearing and sight and minds so that you
might be grateful (78) Have they not seen the birds poised in mid-air?
Nothing holds them up save (the power of) God. Surely in that are signs
for a people who believe (79) And God has made for you your houses a
place of rest. And from the skins of cattle, houses which you find light
(to carry) when you travel and when you camp. And from their wool
and their fur and their hair, furnishings and comfort for a while (80)
And God has made for you shade from what He has created, and he has
made places of refuge for you in the mountains. And He has made garments for you to protect you from the heat and garments to protect
you from your own violence. Thus does He complete His blessings unto
you so that you might surrender (unto Him) (81)

Al-Nahl (The Bee) 16:78-81

إِنَّ اللَّهَ يَأْمُرُ بِالْعَدْلِ وَالْإِحْسَانِ وَإِيتَاءِ ذِي الْقُرْبَىٰ وَيَنْهَىٰ عَنِ الْفَحْشَاءِ وَالْمُنْكَرِ وَالْبَغْيِ ۚ يَعِظُكُمْ لَعَلَّكُمْ تَذَكَّرُونَ ﴿٩٠﴾ ﴿النحل﴾

Truly God commands justice, virtue, and generosity towards kinsfolk, and forbids all that is shameful, immoral and oppressive. He exhorts you so that you might take heed (90)

Al-Nahl (The Bee) 16:90

وَلَوْ شَاءَ اللَّهُ لَجَعَلَكُمْ أُمَّةً وَاحِدَةً وَلَكِنْ يُضِلُّ مَنْ يَشَاءُ وَيَهْدِي مَنْ يَشَاءُ ۚ
وَلَتُسْأَلُنَّ عَمَّا كُنْتُمْ تَعْمَلُونَ ﴿٩٣﴾ ﴿النحل﴾

Had God willed, He could have made you one nation. But He leaves to
stray whoever He will and guides whoever He will. And you shall surely
be questioned about what you used to do (93)

Al-Nahl (The Bee) 16:93

وَلَا تَشْتَرُوا بِعَهْدِ اللَّهِ ثَمَنًا قَلِيلًا ۚ إِنَّمَا عِنْدَ اللَّهِ هُوَ خَيْرٌ لَكُمْ إِنْ كُنْتُمْ

تَعْلَمُونَ ﴿٩٥﴾ ﴿النحل﴾

And do not trade the oath with God for a trivial price. Truly that which is with God is far better for you, if only you knew (95)

Al-Nahl (The Bee) 16:95

مَا عِنْدَكُمْ يَنْفَدُ ۛ وَمَا عِنْدَ اللَّهِ بَاقٍ ۗ وَلَنَجْزِيَنَّ الَّذِينَ صَبَرُوا أَجْرَهُمْ بِأَحْسَنِ مَا كَانُوا يَعْمَلُونَ ﴿٩٦﴾ ﴿النحل﴾

That which you have will end, but that which God has is everlasting. And verily We shall reward those who are steadfast in accordance to the best of what they used to do (96)

Al-Nahl (The Bee) 16:96

مَنْ عَمِلَ صَالِحًا مِنْ ذَكَرٍ أَوْ أُنْثَىٰ وَهُوَ مُؤْمِنٌ فَلَنُحْيِيَنَّهُ حَيَاةً طَيِّبَةً ۖ وَلَنَجْزِيَنَّهُمْ أَجْرَهُمْ بِأَحْسَنِ مَا كَانُوا يَعْمَلُونَ ﴿٩٧﴾ ﴿النحل﴾

Whoever performs righteous deeds; whether male or female, and is a believer, We shall give them a good life and We shall reward them in accordance to the best of what they used to do (97)

Al-Nahl (The Bee) 16:97

فَإِذَا قَرَأْتَ الْقُرْآنَ فَاسْتَعِذْ بِاللَّهِ مِنَ الشَّيْطَانِ الرَّجِيمِ ﴿٩٨﴾ إِنَّهُ لَيْسَ لَهُ سُلْطَانٌ عَلَى الَّذِينَ آمَنُوا وَعَلَىٰ رَبِّهِمْ يَتَوَكَّلُونَ ﴿٩٩﴾ ﴿النحل﴾

So when you recite the Qur'an, seek refuge in God from Satan the outcast (98) Truly he has no power over those who believe and trust in their Lord (99)

Al-Nahl (The Bee) 16:98-99

قُلْ نَزَّلَهُ رُوحُ الْقُدُسِ مِنْ رَبِّكَ بِالْحَقِّ لِيُثَبِّتَ الَّذِينَ آمَنُوا وَهُدًى وَبُشْرَىٰ لِلْمُسْلِمِينَ ﴿١٠٢﴾ ﴿النحل﴾

Say, "The Holy Spirit has brought it down (the Revelation) from thy Lord with the truth, to strengthen (the faith of) those who believe, and as guidance and glad tidings for those who surrender" (102)

Al-Nahl (The Bee) 16:102

وَلَا تَقُولُوا لِمَا تَصِفُ أَلْسِنَتُكُمُ الْكَذِبَ هَٰذَا حَلَالٌ وَهَٰذَا حَرَامٌ لِتَفْتَرُوا عَلَى اللَّهِ الْكَذِبَ ۚ إِنَّ الَّذِينَ يَفْتَرُونَ عَلَى اللَّهِ الْكَذِبَ لَا يُفْلِحُونَ ﴿١١٦﴾

﴿النحل﴾

And do not utter falsehoods by letting your tongues assert "This is lawful and that is forbidden", such that you fabricate a lie against God. Truly those who fabricate lies against God will not prosper (116)

Al-Nahl (The Bee) 16:116

ادْعُ إِلَى سَبِيلِ رَبِّكَ بِالْحِكْمَةِ وَالْمَوْعِظَةِ الْحَسَنَةِ ـ وَجَادِلْهُمْ بِالَّتِي هِيَ
أَحْسَنُ ـ إِنَّ رَبَّكَ هُوَ أَعْلَمُ بِمَنْ ضَلَّ عَنْ سَبِيلِهِ ـ وَهُوَ أَعْلَمُ بِالْمُهْتَدِينَ
﴿١٢٥﴾ ﴿النحل﴾

Call (people) unto the way of thy Lord with wisdom and beautiful preaching. Reason with them in the most courteous manner. Truly, thy Lord knows best who strays from His path, and He knows best who is rightly guided (125)

Al-Nahl (The Bee) 16:125

وَإِنْ عَاقَبْتُمْ فَعَاقِبُوا بِمِثْلِ مَا عُوقِبْتُمْ بِهِۦ وَلَئِنْ صَبَرْتُمْ لَهُوَ خَيْرٌ لِلصَّابِرِينَ

﴿١٢٦﴾ وَاصْبِرْ وَمَا صَبْرُكَ إِلَّا بِاللَّهِ ۚ وَلَا تَحْزَنْ عَلَيْهِمْ وَلَا تَكُ فِي ضَيْقٍ مِمَّا

يَمْكُرُونَ ﴿١٢٧﴾ إِنَّ اللَّهَ مَعَ الَّذِينَ اتَّقَوْا وَالَّذِينَ هُم مُّحْسِنُونَ ﴿١٢٨﴾

﴿النحل﴾

And if you respond (to an attack), then respond with the same extent that you were afflicted. But if you endure patiently, it is better for the patient (126) So be patient, and thy patience is only with (the help of) God. And grieve not over them, nor be distressed by what they plot (127) Truly God is with those who are mindful of Him and those who are virtuous (128)

Al-Nahl (The Bee) 16:126-128

إِنَّ هٰذَا الْقُرْآنَ يَهْدِي لِلَّتِي هِيَ أَقْوَمُ وَيُبَشِّرُ الْمُؤْمِنِينَ الَّذِينَ يَعْمَلُونَ

الصَّالِحَاتِ أَنَّ لَهُمْ أَجْرًا كَبِيرًا ﴿٩﴾ ﴿الإسراء﴾

Truly this Qur'an guides towards that which is most upright, and gives glad tidings to the believers who perform righteous deeds that theirs shall be a great reward (9)

Al-Isra' (The Night Journey) 17:9

وَكُلَّ إِنْسَانٍ أَلْزَمْنَاهُ طَائِرَهُ فِي عُنُقِهِ ۦ وَنُخْرِجُ لَهُ يَوْمَ الْقِيَامَةِ كِتَابًا يَلْقَاهُ

مَنْشُورًا ﴿١٣﴾ اقْرَأْ كِتَابَكَ كَفَىٰ بِنَفْسِكَ الْيَوْمَ عَلَيْكَ حَسِيبًا ﴿١٤﴾ مَنِ

اهْتَدَىٰ فَإِنَّمَا يَهْتَدِي لِنَفْسِهِ ۦ وَمَنْ ضَلَّ فَإِنَّمَا يَضِلُّ عَلَيْهَا ۚ وَلَا تَزِرُ وَازِرَةٌ وِزْرَ

أُخْرَىٰ ۚ وَمَا كُنَّا مُعَذِّبِينَ حَتَّىٰ نَبْعَثَ رَسُولًا ﴿١٥﴾ ﴿الإسراء﴾

And every human being's destiny We have fastened to his neck, and We shall bring forth for him on the Day of Resurrection a record he will find wide open (13) (He will be told:) "Read your (own) record! On this Day your soul suffices as a reckoner against you" (14) Whoever chooses to accept guidance does so for his own good, and whoever strays only strays to his own detriment. None shall bear the burden of another. And never would We punish until We have sent a messenger (15)

Al-Isra' (The Night Journey) 17:13-15

وَمَنْ أَرَادَ الْآخِرَةَ وَسَعَىٰ لَهَا سَعْيَهَا وَهُوَ مُؤْمِنٌ فَأُولَٰئِكَ كَانَ سَعْيُهُم

مَشْكُورًا ﴿١٩﴾ ﴿الإسراء﴾

And whoever desires the Hereafter, and strives for it earnestly, and is a believer, they are the ones whose efforts shall be favoured (19)

Al-Isra' (The Night Journey) 17:19

وَقَضَىٰ رَبُّكَ أَلَّا تَعْبُدُوا إِلَّا إِيَّاهُ وَبِالْوَالِدَيْنِ إِحْسَانًا ۚ إِمَّا يَبْلُغَنَّ عِندَكَ الْكِبَرَ

أَحَدُهُمَا أَوْ كِلَاهُمَا فَلَا تَقُل لَّهُمَا أُفٍّ وَلَا تَنْهَرْهُمَا وَقُل لَّهُمَا قَوْلًا كَرِيمًا

﴿٢٣﴾ وَاخْفِضْ لَهُمَا جَنَاحَ الذُّلِّ مِنَ الرَّحْمَةِ وَقُل رَّبِّ ارْحَمْهُمَا كَمَا

رَبَّيَانِي صَغِيرًا ﴿٢٤﴾ رَّبُّكُمْ أَعْلَمُ بِمَا فِي نُفُوسِكُمْ ۚ إِن تَكُونُوا صَالِحِينَ

فَإِنَّهُ كَانَ لِلْأَوَّابِينَ غَفُورًا ﴿٢٥﴾ وَآتِ ذَا الْقُرْبَىٰ حَقَّهُ وَالْمِسْكِينَ وَابْنَ

السَّبِيلِ وَلَا تُبَذِّرْ تَبْذِيرًا ﴿٢٦﴾ إِنَّ الْمُبَذِّرِينَ كَانُوا إِخْوَانَ الشَّيَاطِينِ ۖ

وَكَانَ الشَّيْطَانُ لِرَبِّهِ كَفُورًا ﴿٢٧﴾ وَإِمَّا تُعْرِضَنَّ عَنْهُمُ ابْتِغَاءَ رَحْمَةٍ مِّن

رَّبِّكَ تَرْجُوهَا فَقُل لَّهُمْ قَوْلًا مَّيْسُورًا ﴿٢٨﴾ وَلَا تَجْعَلْ يَدَكَ مَغْلُولَةً إِلَىٰ

عُنُقِكَ وَلَا تَبْسُطْهَا كُلَّ الْبَسْطِ فَتَقْعُدَ مَلُومًا مَّحْسُورًا ﴿٢٩﴾ إِنَّ رَبَّكَ

يَبْسُطُ الرِّزْقَ لِمَن يَشَاءُ وَيَقْدِرُ ۚ إِنَّهُ كَانَ بِعِبَادِهِ خَبِيرًا بَصِيرًا ﴿٣٠﴾ وَلَا

تَقْتُلُوا أَوْلَادَكُمْ خَشْيَةَ إِمْلَاقٍ ۖ نَّحْنُ نَرْزُقُهُمْ وَإِيَّاكُمْ ۚ إِنَّ قَتْلَهُمْ كَانَ خِطْئًا

كَبِيرًا ﴿٣١﴾ وَلَا تَقْرَبُوا الزِّنَا ۖ إِنَّهُ كَانَ فَاحِشَةً وَسَاءَ سَبِيلًا ﴿٣٢﴾ وَلَا

تَقْتُلُوا النَّفْسَ الَّتِي حَرَّمَ اللَّهُ إِلَّا بِالْحَقِّ ۗ وَمَن قُتِلَ مَظْلُومًا فَقَدْ جَعَلْنَا لِوَلِيِّهِ

سُلْطَانًا فَلَا يُسْرِف فِّي الْقَتْلِ ۖ إِنَّهُ كَانَ مَنصُورًا ﴿٣٣﴾ وَلَا تَقْرَبُوا مَالَ

الْيَتِيمِ إِلَّا بِالَّتِي هِيَ أَحْسَنُ حَتَّىٰ يَبْلُغَ أَشُدَّهُ ۚ وَأَوْفُوا بِالْعَهْدِ ۖ إِنَّ الْعَهْدَ كَانَ

مَسْئُولًا ﴿٣٤﴾ وَأَوْفُوا الْكَيْلَ إِذَا كِلْتُمْ وَزِنُوا بِالْقِسْطَاسِ الْمُسْتَقِيمِ ۚ ذَٰلِكَ

خَيْرٌ وَأَحْسَنُ تَأْوِيلًا ﴿٣٥﴾ وَلَا تَقْفُ مَا لَيْسَ لَكَ بِهِ عِلْمٌ ۚ إِنَّ السَّمْعَ

وَالْبَصَرَ وَالْفُؤَادَ كُلُّ أُولَٰئِكَ كَانَ عَنْهُ مَسْئُولًا ﴿٣٦﴾ وَلَا تَمْشِ فِي الْأَرْضِ

مَرَحًا ۖ إِنَّكَ لَن تَخْرِقَ الْأَرْضَ وَلَن تَبْلُغَ الْجِبَالَ طُولًا ﴿٣٧﴾ كُلُّ ذَٰلِكَ كَانَ

سَيِّئُهُ عِندَ رَبِّكَ مَكْرُوهًا ﴿٣٨﴾ ﴿الإسراء﴾

And your Lord has decreed that you worship none but Him, and be virtuous to your parents. If one or both of them attain old age in your life, say not to them *"Uff"* (a word of contempt) nor scold them, but speak unto them honourably (23) And lower unto them the wing of humility out of mercy, and say "My Lord! Bestow Thy mercy upon them as they cared for me when I was a child" (24) Your Lord knows best what is in your hearts. If you are righteous, then verily He is most forgiving unto those who turn unto Him (25) And give the near of kin their due, and the needy, and the wayfarer and squander not wastefully (26) Truly the squanderers are brothers of Satan, and Satan is ever ungrateful to his Lord (27) But if thou turn away from them, seeking mercy from thy Lord for which you hope, then speak unto them a gentle word (28) And let not thy hand be shackled to thy neck nor let it be open entirely, lest thou should be blamed, destitute (29) Truly thy Lord gives abundant provisions to whoever He will and sparingly to whoever He will. Verily of His servants He is Aware, Seeing (30) Kill not your children, fearing a fall to poverty. We shall provide sustenance for them and for you. Verily the killing of them is a great sin (31) And approach not adultery. Verily it is an abomination and an evil way (32) And take not the life which God has made sacred, save for just cause. Whoever is slain wrongfully, We have given authority unto his heir, but let him not be excessive in taking life. Verily he shall be helped (33) And approach not the wealth of the orphan save with that which is better, until he reaches maturity. And keep the oath, surely the oath will be called to account (34) And give full measure when you measure, and weigh with a true balance. That is better and best in the end (35) And concern yourself not with that which you have no knowledge. Verily, hearing and sight and the heart – all of these will be called into account (on the Day of Judgement) (36) And walk not on the earth arrogantly, surely thou shalt not rend the earth asunder, nor match the mountains in height (37) The evil of all this is hateful unto thy Lord (38)

Al-Isra' (The Night Journey) 17:23-38

إِنَّ عِبَادِي لَيْسَ لَكَ عَلَيْهِمْ سُلْطَانٌ ۚ وَكَفَىٰ بِرَبِّكَ وَكِيلًا ﴿٦٥﴾ ﴿الإسراء﴾

"Truly My servants, thou hast no authority over them." And thy Lord suffices as a Guardian (65)

Al-Isra' (The Night Journey) 17:65

وَلَقَدْ كَرَّمْنَا بَنِي آدَمَ وَحَمَلْنَاهُمْ فِي الْبَرِّ وَالْبَحْرِ وَرَزَقْنَاهُمْ مِنَ الطَّيِّبَاتِ وَفَضَّلْنَاهُمْ عَلَىٰ كَثِيرٍ مِمَّنْ خَلَقْنَا تَفْضِيلًا ﴿٧٠﴾ يَوْمَ نَدْعُو كُلَّ أُنَاسٍ بِإِمَامِهِمْ ۖ فَمَنْ أُوتِيَ كِتَابَهُ بِيَمِينِهِ فَأُولَٰئِكَ يَقْرَءُونَ كِتَابَهُمْ وَلَا يُظْلَمُونَ فَتِيلًا ﴿٧١﴾ ﴿الإسراء﴾

Verily We have honoured the Children of Adam, and We carried them over land and sea. We provided sustenance of good things for them. And We have favoured them above many of those We have created (70) One Day We shall summon all human beings with their leaders, whoever is given their record in their right hand, it is they who shall read their records and they shall not be wronged a shred (71)

Al-Isra' (The Night Journey) 17:70-71

أَقِمِ الصَّلَاةَ لِدُلُوكِ الشَّمْسِ إِلَى غَسَقِ اللَّيْلِ وَقُرْآنَ الْفَجْرِ ۖ إِنَّ قُرْآنَ الْفَجْرِ

كَانَ مَشْهُودًا ﴿٧٨﴾ وَمِنَ اللَّيْلِ فَتَهَجَّدْ بِهِ نَافِلَةً لَكَ عَسَىٰ أَنْ يَبْعَثَكَ رَبُّكَ

مَقَامًا مَحْمُودًا ﴿٧٩﴾ وَقُلْ رَبِّ أَدْخِلْنِي مُدْخَلَ صِدْقٍ وَأَخْرِجْنِي مُخْرَجَ

صِدْقٍ وَاجْعَلْ لِي مِنْ لَدُنْكَ سُلْطَانًا نَصِيرًا ﴿٨٠﴾ وَقُلْ جَاءَ الْحَقُّ وَزَهَقَ

الْبَاطِلُ ۚ إِنَّ الْبَاطِلَ كَانَ زَهُوقًا ﴿٨١﴾ ﴿الإسراء﴾

Perform the prayer from the time the sun is past its zenith till the darkness of the night. And (recite) the Qur'an at dawn – truly the recitation at dawn is ever witnessed (78) And during the night awaken and pray, as an additional contribution from thee, so that your Lord may raise thee to a praised station (79) And say "My Lord! Let me enter in a sincere manner, and let me go forth in a sincere manner, and grant me from Thy presence a sustaining authority" (80) And say "Truth has come and falsehood has perished. Truly falsehood is ever bound to perish" (81)

Al-Isra' (The Night Journey) 17:78-81

وَنُنَزِّلُ مِنَ الْقُرْآنِ مَا هُوَ شِفَاءٌ وَرَحْمَةٌ لِلْمُؤْمِنِينَ ۙ وَلَا يَزِيدُ الظَّالِمِينَ إِلَّا خَسَارًا ﴿٨٢﴾ ﴿الإسراء﴾

And We send down in the Qur'an that which is healing and a mercy for the believers. And it increases the wrongdoers in nothing but loss (82)

Al-Isra' (The Night Journey) 17:82

قُل لَّئِنِ اجْتَمَعَتِ الْإِنسُ وَالْجِنُّ عَلَىٰ أَن يَأْتُوا بِمِثْلِ هَٰذَا الْقُرْآنِ لَا يَأْتُونَ

بِمِثْلِهِ وَلَوْ كَانَ بَعْضُهُمْ لِبَعْضٍ ظَهِيرًا ﴿٨٨﴾ وَلَقَدْ صَرَّفْنَا لِلنَّاسِ فِي هَٰذَا

الْقُرْآنِ مِن كُلِّ مَثَلٍ فَأَبَىٰ أَكْثَرُ النَّاسِ إِلَّا كُفُورًا ﴿٨٩﴾ ﴿الإسراء﴾

Say "Surely if mankind and jinn came together to produce the like of this Qur'an, they could not produce anything like it, even if they helped one another" (88) And indeed We have set out every kind of parable for mankind in this Qur'an. Yet most mankind refuse to accept and disbelieve (89)

Al-Isra' (The Night Journey) 17:88-89

وَبِالْحَقِّ أَنْزَلْنَاهُ وَبِالْحَقِّ نَزَلَ ۗ وَمَا أَرْسَلْنَاكَ إِلَّا مُبَشِّرًا وَنَذِيرًا ﴿١٠٥﴾

﴿الإسراء﴾

With the truth We sent it down (the Qur'an), and with truth it descended. And We sent thee (Muhammad) save as a bearer of glad tidings and as a warner (105)

Al-Isra' (The Night Journey) 17:105

قُلِ ادْعُوا اللَّهَ أَوِ ادْعُوا الرَّحْمَنَ ۖ أَيًّا مَا تَدْعُوا فَلَهُ الْأَسْمَاءُ الْحُسْنَىٰ ۚ وَلَا

تَجْهَرْ بِصَلَاتِكَ وَلَا تُخَافِتْ بِهَا وَابْتَغِ بَيْنَ ذَٰلِكَ سَبِيلاً ﴿110﴾ ﴿الإسراء﴾

Say (unto mankind), "Call upon God, or call upon the Compassionate.
By whichever you call upon (it is well), for to Him belong the Most
Beautiful Names. And be neither too loud in your prayer, nor too quiet
therein, but seek a middle way" (110)

Al-Isra' (The Night Journey) 17:110

وَقُلِ الْحَمْدُ لِلَّهِ الَّذِي لَمْ يَتَّخِذْ وَلَدًا وَلَمْ يَكُنْ لَهُ شَرِيكٌ فِي الْمُلْكِ وَلَمْ

يَكُنْ لَهُ وَلِيٌّ مِنَ الذُّلِّ ۖ وَكَبِّرْهُ تَكْبِيرًا ﴿١١١﴾ ﴿الإسراء﴾

And say, "Praise be to God, Who begets no child, and Who has no partner in His sovereignty, nor has He any protector out of weakness." And proclaim His limitless Greatness (111)

Al-Isra' (The Night Journey) 17:111

الْحَمْدُ لِلَّهِ الَّذِي أَنْزَلَ عَلَىٰ عَبْدِهِ الْكِتَابَ وَلَمْ يَجْعَلْ لَهُ عِوَجًا ﴿١﴾ قَيِّمًا

لِيُنْذِرَ بَأْسًا شَدِيدًا مِنْ لَدُنْهُ وَيُبَشِّرَ الْمُؤْمِنِينَ الَّذِينَ يَعْمَلُونَ الصَّالِحَاتِ أَنَّ

لَهُمْ أَجْرًا حَسَنًا ﴿٢﴾ مَاكِثِينَ فِيهِ أَبَدًا ﴿٣﴾ ﴿الكهف﴾

Praise be to God, Who has sent down the Scripture unto His servant, and has not placed therein any variation (of the truth) (1) Unerringly straight (and balanced), so that He may warn of severe punishment-from Him, and to give glad tidings unto the believers who perform righteous deeds that theirs shall be an excellent reward (2) Wherein they shall remain forever (3)

Al-Kahf (The Cave) 18:1-3

إِنَّا جَعَلْنَا مَا عَلَى الْأَرْضِ زِينَةً لَهَا لِنَبْلُوَهُمْ أَيُّهُمْ أَحْسَنُ عَمَلًا ﴿٧﴾

﴿الكهف﴾

Behold, We have adorned what is on the earth with attractive things so that We may test them (people) to find out which of them is most virtuous in deeds (7)

Al-Kahf (The Cave) 18:7

وَاتْلُ مَا أُوحِيَ إِلَيْكَ مِنْ كِتَابِ رَبِّكَ ۖ لَا مُبَدِّلَ لِكَلِمَاتِهِ وَلَنْ تَجِدَ مِنْ دُونِهِ مُلْتَحَدًا ﴿٢٧﴾ ﴿الكهف﴾

And recite what has been revealed unto thee from the Scripture of thy Lord. None can change His Words and thou wilt find no refuge other than Him (27)

Al-Kahf (The Cave) 18:27

وَاصْبِرْ نَفْسَكَ مَعَ الَّذِينَ يَدْعُونَ رَبَّهُمْ بِالْغَدَاةِ وَالْعَشِيِّ يُرِيدُونَ وَجْهَهُ ۖ وَلَا

تَعْدُ عَيْنَاكَ عَنْهُمْ تُرِيدُ زِينَةَ الْحَيَاةِ الدُّنْيَا ۖ وَلَا تُطِعْ مَنْ أَغْفَلْنَا قَلْبَهُ عَنْ

ذِكْرِنَا وَاتَّبَعَ هَوَاهُ وَكَانَ أَمْرُهُ فُرُطًا ﴿٢٨﴾ وَقُلِ الْحَقُّ مِنْ رَبِّكُمْ ۖ فَمَنْ شَاءَ

فَلْيُؤْمِنْ وَمَنْ شَاءَ فَلْيَكْفُرْ ۚ إِنَّا أَعْتَدْنَا لِلظَّالِمِينَ نَارًا أَحَاطَ بِهِمْ سُرَادِقُهَا ۚ

وَإِنْ يَسْتَغِيثُوا يُغَاثُوا بِمَاءٍ كَالْمُهْلِ يَشْوِي الْوُجُوهَ ۚ بِئْسَ الشَّرَابُ وَسَاءَتْ

مُرْتَفَقًا ﴿٢٩﴾ إِنَّ الَّذِينَ آمَنُوا وَعَمِلُوا الصَّالِحَاتِ إِنَّا لَا نُضِيعُ أَجْرَ مَنْ

أَحْسَنَ عَمَلًا ﴿٣٠﴾ ﴿الكهف﴾

And contain thyself in patience with those who call upon their Lord morning and evening, seeking His Countenance; and let not thine eyes overlook them, desiring the adornment of this worldly life; and obey not those whose heart We have made heedless of Our remembrance, one who follows his own desires and whose case has been abandoned (28) And say, "The truth is from your Lord! So whoever wills, let him believe, and whoever wills, let him reject it." Verily We have prepared for the wrongdoers a Fire that will encompass them from all sides. And if they plead for relief, they will be showered with water like molten lead that will scald their faces – how dreadful a drink indeed, and how terrible a place to rest! (29) As for those who believe and perform righteous deeds, truly We do not fail to reward those who do virtuous deeds (30)

Al-Kahf (The Cave) 18:28-30

إِنَّ الَّذِينَ آمَنُوا وَعَمِلُوا الصَّالِحَاتِ كَانَتْ لَهُمْ جَنَّاتُ الْفِرْدَوْسِ نُزُلًا

﴿١٠٧﴾ خَالِدِينَ فِيهَا لَا يَبْغُونَ عَنْهَا حِوَلًا ﴿١٠٨﴾ ﴿الكهف﴾

Truly those who believe and perform righteous deeds, theirs shall be the Gardens of Paradise as a welcome (107) Abiding therein, with no desire to leave (108)

Al-Kahf (The Cave) 18:107-108

قُلْ لَوْ كَانَ الْبَحْرُ مِدَادًا لِكَلِمَاتِ رَبِّي لَنَفِدَ الْبَحْرُ قَبْلَ أَنْ تَنْفَدَ كَلِمَاتُ

رَبِّي وَلَوْ جِئْنَا بِمِثْلِهِ مَدَدًا ﴿١٠٩﴾ ﴿الكهف﴾

Say "If the sea were ink for the Words of my Lord, verily sooner would the sea be exhausted before the Words of my Lord were exhausted, even if We were to add to it sea upon sea" (109)

Al-Kahf (The Cave) 18:109

إِلَّا مَنْ تَابَ وَآمَنَ وَعَمِلَ صَالِحًا فَأُولَٰئِكَ يَدْخُلُونَ الْجَنَّةَ وَلَا يُظْلَمُونَ شَيْئًا

﴿٦٠﴾ جَنَّاتِ عَدْنٍ الَّتِي وَعَدَ الرَّحْمَٰنُ عِبَادَهُ بِالْغَيْبِ ۚ إِنَّهُ كَانَ وَعْدُهُ

مَأْتِيًّا ﴿٦١﴾ لَا يَسْمَعُونَ فِيهَا لَغْوًا إِلَّا سَلَامًا ۖ وَلَهُمْ رِزْقُهُمْ فِيهَا بُكْرَةً وَعَشِيًّا

﴿٦٢﴾ تِلْكَ الْجَنَّةُ الَّتِي نُورِثُ مِنْ عِبَادِنَا مَنْ كَانَ تَقِيًّا ﴿٦٣﴾ ﴿مريم﴾

Save those who repent and believe and performs righteous deeds. It is they who shall enter paradise, and they shall not be wronged in any way (60) Gardens of Eden, which the Compassionate has promised to His servants in the Unseen. Verily His Promise must be fulfilled (61) They hear therein no frivolity, but only (tidings of) Peace. And therein they shall have their sustenance, morning and evening (62) This is the Paradise which We shall grant as a heritage unto Our servants who were devout (63)

Maryam (Mary) 19:60-63

وَمَا نَتَنَزَّلُ إِلَّا بِأَمْرِ رَبِّكَ ۖ لَهُ مَا بَيْنَ أَيْدِينَا وَمَا خَلْفَنَا وَمَا بَيْنَ ذَٰلِكَ ۚ وَمَا

كَانَ رَبُّكَ نَسِيًّا ﴿٦٤﴾ رَبُّ السَّمَاوَاتِ وَالْأَرْضِ وَمَا بَيْنَهُمَا فَاعْبُدْهُ وَاصْطَبِرْ

لِعِبَادَتِهِ ۚ هَلْ تَعْلَمُ لَهُ سَمِيًّا ﴿٦٥﴾ ﴿مريم﴾

(The angels say) "We do not descend (with revelation), save by the Command of thy Lord. Unto Him belongs all that is before us and all that is behind us, and whatever is between that, and thy Lord is not forgetful (64) Lord of the heavens and the earth and whatever is between them. So worship Him and be steadfast in His worship. Dost thou know one that can be named alongside Him?" (65)

Maryam (Mary) 19:64-65

إِنَّ الَّذِينَ آمَنُوا وَعَمِلُوا الصَّالِحَاتِ سَيَجْعَلُ لَهُمُ الرَّحْمَنُ وُدًّا ﴿٩٦﴾

﴿مريم﴾

Truly those who believe and perform righteous deeds, the Compassionate shall endow with love (96)

Maryam (Mary) 19:96

مَا أَنْزَلْنَا عَلَيْكَ الْقُرْآنَ لِتَشْقَىٰ ﴿٢﴾ إِلَّا تَذْكِرَةً لِمَنْ يَخْشَىٰ ﴿٣﴾ تَنْزِيلًا

مِمَّنْ خَلَقَ الْأَرْضَ وَالسَّمَاوَاتِ الْعُلَى ﴿٤﴾ ﴿طه﴾

We have not sent down the Qur'an unto thee (Muhammad) for thy distress (2) But as a reminder for those who are in awe (of God) (3) A revelation from the One Who created the earth and the high heavens (4)

Tā Hā (Ta Ha) 20:2-4

الرَّحْمٰنُ عَلَى الْعَرْشِ اسْتَوَىٰ ﴿٥﴾ لَهُ مَا فِي السَّمَاوَاتِ وَمَا فِي الْأَرْضِ وَمَا بَيْنَهُمَا وَمَا تَحْتَ الثَّرَىٰ ﴿٦﴾ وَإِنْ تَجْهَرْ بِالْقَوْلِ فَإِنَّهُ يَعْلَمُ السِّرَّ وَأَخْفَى ﴿٧﴾ اللَّهُ لاَ إِلَهَ إِلاَّ هُوَ لَهُ الْأَسْمَاءُ الْحُسْنَىٰ ﴿٨﴾ ﴿طه﴾

The Compassionate, established on the Throne (5) Unto Him belongs all that is in the heavens and all that is on the earth, and all that is between them, and all that is beneath the soil (6) And if thou speakest aloud, verily He knows what is secret and what is yet more hidden (7) God, there is no god but Him. To Him belong the Most Beautiful Names (8)

Tā Hā (Ta Ha) 20:5-8

قَالَ رَبِّ اشْرَحْ لِي صَدْرِي ﴿٢٥﴾ وَيَسِّرْ لِي أَمْرِي ﴿٢٦﴾ وَاحْلُلْ عُقْدَةً
مِنْ لِسَانِي ﴿٢٧﴾ يَفْقَهُوا قَوْلِي ﴿٢٨﴾ ﴿طه﴾

(Moses) said "My Lord! Open my heart (25) And ease my task for me (26) And loosen a knot from my tongue (27) So they may understand what I say (28)

Tā Hā (Ta Ha) 20:25-28

قَالَ اهْبِطَا مِنْهَا جَمِيعًا بَعْضُكُمْ لِبَعْضٍ عَدُوٌّ فَإِمَّا يَأْتِيَنَّكُمْ مِنِّي هُدًى فَمَنِ اتَّبَعَ هُدَايَ فَلَا يَضِلُّ وَلَا يَشْقَىٰ ﴿١٢٣﴾ ﴿طه﴾

He said "Go down hence, both of you (from the Garden); all together, each of you an enemy to the other. And if guidance should come unto you from Me, then whoever follows My guidance shall not go astray nor fall into misery" (123)

Tā Hā (Ta Ha) 20:123

فَاصْبِرْ عَلَىٰ مَا يَقُولُونَ وَسَبِّحْ بِحَمْدِ رَبِّكَ قَبْلَ طُلُوعِ الشَّمْسِ وَقَبْلَ غُرُوبِهَا

وَمِنْ آنَاءِ اللَّيْلِ فَسَبِّحْ وَأَطْرَافَ النَّهَارِ لَعَلَّكَ تَرْضَىٰ ﴿١٣٠﴾ وَلَا تَمُدَّنَّ

عَيْنَيْكَ إِلَىٰ مَا مَتَّعْنَا بِهِ أَزْوَاجًا مِنْهُمْ زَهْرَةَ الْحَيَاةِ الدُّنْيَا لِنَفْتِنَهُمْ فِيهِ وَرِزْقُ

رَبِّكَ خَيْرٌ وَأَبْقَىٰ ﴿١٣١﴾ وَأْمُرْ أَهْلَكَ بِالصَّلَاةِ وَاصْطَبِرْ عَلَيْهَا لَا نَسْأَلُكَ

رِزْقًا نَحْنُ نَرْزُقُكَ وَالْعَاقِبَةُ لِلتَّقْوَىٰ ﴿١٣٢﴾ ﴿طه﴾

So endure patiently with what they say, and glorify the praise of thy
Lord before the rising of the sun and before its setting, and in the
hours of the night glorify (Him), and at the ends of the day, that thou
may be content (130) And strain not thine eyes (with longing) toward
the splendour that We may have granted others to enjoy in the life of
this world; through which We test them. For the provision of thy Lord
is better and more enduring (131) And instruct your people to pray and
be steadfast therein. We do not ask of thee to provide sustenance; We
provide sustenance for thee. And the reward (of the Hereafter) belongs
to the devout (132)

Tā Hā (Ta Ha) 20:130-132

فَمَنْ يَعْمَلْ مِنَ الصَّالِحَاتِ وَهُوَ مُؤْمِنٌ فَلَا كُفْرَانَ لِسَعْيِهِ وَإِنَّا لَهُ كَاتِبُونَ ﴿٩٤﴾ ﴿الأنبياء﴾

Whoever performs righteous deeds and is a believer, there shall be no rejection for his endeavour, and surely We shall record it for him (in his favour) (94)

Al-Anbiyā (The Prophets) 21:94

إِنَّ اللَّهَ يُدْخِلُ الَّذِينَ آمَنُوا وَعَمِلُوا الصَّالِحَاتِ جَنَّاتٍ تَجْرِي مِنْ تَحْتِهَا الْأَنْهَارُ يُحَلَّوْنَ فِيهَا مِنْ أَسَاوِرَ مِنْ ذَهَبٍ وَلُؤْلُؤًا ۖ وَلِبَاسُهُمْ فِيهَا حَرِيرٌ ﴿٢٣﴾ ﴿الحج﴾

Truly God will admit those who believe and perform righteous deeds into Gardens beneath which rivers flow. Adorned therein with bracelets of gold and pearl, and therein their garments will be of silk (23)

Al-Hajj (The Pilgrimage) 22:23

إِنَّ اللَّهَ يُدَافِعُ عَنِ الَّذِينَ آمَنُوا ۗ إِنَّ اللَّهَ لَا يُحِبُّ كُلَّ خَوَّانٍ كَفُورٍ ﴿٣٨﴾

﴿الحج﴾

Truly God will defend those who believe. Truly God does not love any unfaithful traitor (38)

Al-Hajj (The Pilgrimage) 22:38

فَالَّذِينَ آمَنُوا وَعَمِلُوا الصَّالِحَاتِ لَهُم مَّغْفِرَةٌ وَرِزْقٌ كَرِيمٌ ﴿٥٠﴾ ﴿الحج﴾

Those who believe and perform righteous deeds, for them shall be forgiveness and a generous provision (50)

Al-Hajj (The Pilgrimage) 22:50

أَلَمْ تَرَ أَنَّ اللَّهَ أَنْزَلَ مِنَ السَّمَاءِ مَاءً فَتُصْبِحُ الْأَرْضُ مُخْضَرَّةً ۚ إِنَّ اللَّهَ

لَطِيفٌ خَبِيرٌ ﴿٦٣﴾ لَهُ مَا فِي السَّمَاوَاتِ وَمَا فِي الْأَرْضِ ۚ وَإِنَّ اللَّهَ لَهُوَ

الْغَنِيُّ الْحَمِيدُ ﴿٦٤﴾ ﴿الحج﴾

Have you not considered how God sends down water from the sky whereupon the earth becomes green? Truly God is Gracious, All-Aware (63) To Him belongs all that is in the heavens and all that is on the earth. And God is truly the Self-Sufficient, the Praised (64)

Al-Hajj (The Pilgrimage) 22:63-64

أَلَمْ تَرَ أَنَّ اللَّهَ سَخَّرَ لَكُمْ مَا فِي الْأَرْضِ وَالْفُلْكَ تَجْرِي فِي الْبَحْرِ بِأَمْرِهِ

وَيُمْسِكُ السَّمَاءَ أَنْ تَقَعَ عَلَى الْأَرْضِ إِلَّا بِإِذْنِهِ ۗ إِنَّ اللَّهَ بِالنَّاسِ لَرَءُوفٌ

رَحِيمٌ ﴿٦٥﴾ ﴿الحج﴾

Have you not considered how God has made everything that is on the earth subservient to you and the ships that sail upon the sea by His Command? And He holds the sky lest it fall upon the earth, save by His Leave. Truly God is Compassionate and Merciful to mankind (65)

Al-Hajj (The Pilgrimage) 22:65

قَدْ أَفْلَحَ الْمُؤْمِنُونَ ﴿١﴾ الَّذِينَ هُمْ فِي صَلَاتِهِمْ خَاشِعُونَ ﴿٢﴾ وَالَّذِينَ هُمْ عَنِ اللَّغْوِ مُعْرِضُونَ ﴿٣﴾ وَالَّذِينَ هُمْ لِلزَّكَاةِ فَاعِلُونَ ﴿٤﴾ وَالَّذِينَ هُمْ لِفُرُوجِهِمْ حَافِظُونَ ﴿٥﴾ إِلَّا عَلَىٰ أَزْوَاجِهِمْ أَوْ مَا مَلَكَتْ أَيْمَانُهُمْ فَإِنَّهُمْ غَيْرُ مَلُومِينَ ﴿٦﴾ فَمَنِ ابْتَغَىٰ وَرَاءَ ذَٰلِكَ فَأُولَٰئِكَ هُمُ الْعَادُونَ ﴿٧﴾ وَالَّذِينَ هُمْ لِأَمَانَاتِهِمْ وَعَهْدِهِمْ رَاعُونَ ﴿٨﴾ وَالَّذِينَ هُمْ عَلَىٰ صَلَوَاتِهِمْ يُحَافِظُونَ ﴿٩﴾ أُولَٰئِكَ هُمُ الْوَارِثُونَ ﴿١٠﴾ الَّذِينَ يَرِثُونَ الْفِرْدَوْسَ هُمْ فِيهَا خَالِدُونَ ﴿١١﴾ ﴿المؤمنون﴾

Successful indeed are the believers (1) Who humble themselves in their prayers (2) And who shun frivolity (3) And who give the alms (4) And who guard their modesty (5) Save from their spouses or those whom their right hands possess, for this they are not to blame (6) But those who seek beyond that, they are the transgressors (7) And who are faithful to their trust and their oath (8) And who are mindful of their prayers (9) It is they who are the heirs (10) Who shall inherit paradise, abiding therein (11)

Al-Mu-minūn (The Believers) 23:1-11

وَالَّذِينَ يُؤْتُونَ مَا آتَوا وَقُلُوبُهُمْ وَجِلَةٌ أَنَّهُمْ إِلَىٰ رَبِّهِمْ رَاجِعُونَ ﴿٦٠﴾ أُولَٰئِكَ يُسَارِعُونَ فِي الْخَيْرَاتِ وَهُمْ لَهَا سَابِقُونَ ﴿٦١﴾ ﴿المؤمنون﴾

And those who give what they give (of charity) with hearts full of fear that they shall return to their Lord (60) It is they who hasten in doing good deeds, and are first in attaining them (61)

Al-Mu-minūn (The Believers) 23:60-61

240

وَلَا نُكَلِّفُ نَفْسًا إِلَّا وُسْعَهَا ـ وَلَدَيْنَا كِتَابٌ يَنْطِقُ بِالْحَقِّ ۽ وَهُمْ لَا يُظْلَمُونَ

﴿٦٢﴾ ﴿المؤمنون﴾

And We burden no soul beyond what it can bear, and with Us is a Record that speaks in truth. And they shall not be wronged (62)

Al-Mu-minūn (The Believers) 23:62

أَفَحَسِبْتُمْ أَنَّمَا خَلَقْنَاكُمْ عَبَثًا وَأَنَّكُمْ إِلَيْنَا لَا تُرْجَعُونَ ﴿١١٥﴾ فَتَعَالَى اللَّهُ

الْمَلِكُ الْحَقُّ ۖ لَا إِلَهَ إِلَّا هُوَ رَبُّ الْعَرْشِ الْكَرِيمِ ﴿١١٦﴾ ﴿المؤمنون﴾

"Did you then think that We created you in vain, and that you would not be returned to Us?" (115) So, exalted is God, the True King; there is no god but Him, Lord of the Gracious Throne (116)

Al-Mu-minūn (The Believers) 23:115-116

وَقُلْ رَبِّ اغْفِرْ وَارْحَمْ وَأَنْتَ خَيْرُ الرَّاحِمِينَ ﴿١١٨﴾ ﴿المؤمنون﴾

And say, "My Lord! Forgive and bestow Thy mercy, for Thou art the best bestower of mercy!" (118)

Al-Mu-minūn (The Believers) 23:118

يَا أَيُّهَا الَّذِينَ آمَنُوا لَا تَتَّبِعُوا خُطُوَاتِ الشَّيْطَانِ ۚ وَمَنْ يَتَّبِعْ خُطُوَاتِ
الشَّيْطَانِ فَإِنَّهُ يَأْمُرُ بِالْفَحْشَاءِ وَالْمُنْكَرِ ۚ وَلَوْلَا فَضْلُ اللَّهِ عَلَيْكُمْ وَرَحْمَتُهُ
مَا زَكَىٰ مِنْكُمْ مِنْ أَحَدٍ أَبَدًا وَلَٰكِنَّ اللَّهَ يُزَكِّي مَنْ يَشَاءُ ۚ وَاللَّهُ سَمِيعٌ عَلِيمٌ
﴿٢١﴾ ﴿النور﴾

O you who believe! Follow not the footsteps of Satan! And whoever follows the footsteps of Satan, truly he urges to indecency and immorality. And were it not for God's favour upon you, and His mercy, not one of you would ever attain purity. But God purifies whoever He will, and God is Hearing, Knowing (21)

Al-Nūr (The Light) 24:21

وَلَا يَأْتَلِ أُولُو الْفَضْلِ مِنْكُمْ وَالسَّعَةِ أَنْ يُؤْتُوا أُولِي الْقُرْبَى وَالْمَسَاكِينَ وَالْمُهَاجِرِينَ فِي سَبِيلِ اللَّهِ ۖ وَلْيَعْفُوا وَلْيَصْفَحُوا ۗ أَلَا تُحِبُّونَ أَنْ يَغْفِرَ اللَّهُ لَكُمْ ۗ وَاللَّهُ غَفُورٌ رَحِيمٌ ﴿٢٢﴾ ﴿النور﴾

And let not those who have been blessed with abundance and means among you swear not to give to the near of kin and to the needy and those who emigrated in God's cause. Let them pardon and forbear. Do you not desire that God should forgive you? God is Forgiving, Merciful (22)

Al-Nūr (The Light) 24:22

الْخَبِيثَاتُ لِلْخَبِيثِينَ وَالْخَبِيثُونَ لِلْخَبِيثَاتِ ـ وَالطَّيِّبَاتُ لِلطَّيِّبِينَ وَالطَّيِّبُونَ

لِلطَّيِّبَاتِ ۚ أُولَٰئِكَ مُبَرَّءُونَ مِمَّا يَقُولُونَ ـ لَهُم مَّغْفِرَةٌ وَرِزْقٌ كَرِيمٌ ﴿٢٦﴾

﴿النور﴾

Wicked women are for wicked men, and wicked men for wicked women. Good women are for good men, and good men for good women; they are innocent of what people say: For them is pardon and a generous provision (26)

Al-Nūr (The Light) 24:26

اللَّهُ نُورُ السَّمَاوَاتِ وَالْأَرْضِ، مَثَلُ نُورِهِ كَمِشْكَاةٍ فِيهَا مِصْبَاحٌ ـ الْمِصْبَاحُ

فِي زُجَاجَةٍ ـ الزُّجَاجَةُ كَأَنَّهَا كَوْكَبٌ دُرِّيٌّ يُوقَدُ مِنْ شَجَرَةٍ مُبَارَكَةٍ زَيْتُونَةٍ

لَا شَرْقِيَّةٍ وَلَا غَرْبِيَّةٍ يَكَادُ زَيْتُهَا يُضِيءُ وَلَوْ لَمْ تَمْسَسْهُ نَارٌ، نُورٌ عَلَى نُورٍ

يَهْدِي اللَّهُ لِنُورِهِ مَنْ يَشَاءُ، وَيَضْرِبُ اللَّهُ الْأَمْثَالَ لِلنَّاسِ ـ وَاللَّهُ بِكُلِّ شَيْءٍ

عَلِيمٌ ﴿٣٥﴾ ﴿النور﴾

God is the Light of the heavens and the earth. The parable of His Light
is that of a niche, in which there is a lamp. The lamp is (enclosed) in
a glass. The glass is like a shining star lit from a blessed olive tree,
neither of the East nor of the West. Its oil gives light (so bright) even
though fire had not touched it. Light upon Light! God guides unto His
Light whomever He will and God sets forth parables for mankind, and
God is Knower of all things (35)

Al-Nūr (The Light) 24:35

رِجَالٌ لَا تُلْهِيهِمْ تِجَارَةٌ وَلَا بَيْعٌ عَنْ ذِكْرِ اللَّهِ وَإِقَامِ الصَّلَاةِ وَإِيتَاءِ الزَّكَاةِ ﱟ

يَخَافُونَ يَوْمًا تَتَقَلَّبُ فِيهِ الْقُلُوبُ وَالْأَبْصَارُ ﴿٣٧﴾ لِيَجْزِيَهُمُ اللَّهُ أَحْسَنَ

مَا عَمِلُوا وَيَزِيدَهُمْ مِنْ فَضْلِهِ وَاللَّهُ يَرْزُقُ مَنْ يَشَاءُ بِغَيْرِ حِسَابٍ ﴿٣٨﴾

﴿النور﴾

Men who neither commerce nor profit divert them from the remembrance of God, the performance of prayer, and the giving of alms, fearing a day when hearts and eyes will be transformed (37) That God may reward them for the best of what they have done, and increase them from His Bounty. And God provides for whomever He will without reckoning (38)

Al-Nūr (The Light) 24:37-38

وَلِلَّهِ مُلْكُ السَّمَاوَاتِ وَالْأَرْضِ ـ وَإِلَى اللَّهِ الْمَصِيرُ ﴿٤٢﴾ ﴿النور﴾

And unto God belongs sovereignty over the heavens and the earth, and unto God is the journey's end (42)

Al-Nūr (The Light) 24:42

لَقَدْ أَنْزَلْنَا آيَاتٍ مُبَيِّنَاتٍ ۚ وَاللَّهُ يَهْدِي مَنْ يَشَاءُ إِلَىٰ صِرَاطٍ مُسْتَقِيمٍ ﴿٤٦﴾

﴿النور﴾

Indeed, We have sent down clear signs and God guides whomever He will unto a straight path (46)

Al-Nūr (The Light) 24:46

وَمَنْ يُطِعِ اللَّهَ وَرَسُولَهُ وَيَخْشَ اللَّهَ وَيَتَّقْهِ فَأُولَٰئِكَ هُمُ الْفَائِزُونَ ﴿٥٢﴾

﴿النور﴾

Whoever obeys God and His Messenger, and who is in awe of God and is conscious of Him, it is they who shall triumph (52)

Al-Nūr (The Light) 24:52

تَبَارَكَ الَّذِي جَعَلَ فِي السَّمَاءِ بُرُوجًا وَجَعَلَ فِيهَا سِرَاجًا وَقَمَرًا مُنِيرًا

﴿٦١﴾ وَهُوَ الَّذِي جَعَلَ اللَّيْلَ وَالنَّهَارَ خِلْفَةً لِمَنْ أَرَادَ أَنْ يَذَّكَّرَ أَوْ أَرَادَ

شُكُورًا ﴿٦٢﴾ ﴿الفرقان﴾

Blessed is He Who placed constellations in the sky and placed among them a lamp and a shining moon (61) And it is He Who appointed the night and the day in succession, for whoever desires to reflect or desires to give thanks (62)

Al-Furqān (The Distinguisher) 25:61-62

وَعِبَادُ الرَّحْمَٰنِ الَّذِينَ يَمْشُونَ عَلَى الْأَرْضِ هَوْنًا وَإِذَا خَاطَبَهُمُ الْجَاهِلُونَ قَالُوا سَلَامًا ﴿٦٣﴾ وَالَّذِينَ يَبِيتُونَ لِرَبِّهِمْ سُجَّدًا وَقِيَامًا ﴿٦٤﴾ وَالَّذِينَ يَقُولُونَ رَبَّنَا اصْرِفْ عَنَّا عَذَابَ جَهَنَّمَ ۖ إِنَّ عَذَابَهَا كَانَ غَرَامًا ﴿٦٥﴾ إِنَّهَا سَاءَتْ مُسْتَقَرًّا وَمُقَامًا ﴿٦٦﴾ وَالَّذِينَ إِذَا أَنْفَقُوا لَمْ يُسْرِفُوا وَلَمْ يَقْتُرُوا وَكَانَ بَيْنَ ذَٰلِكَ قَوَامًا ﴿٦٧﴾ وَالَّذِينَ لَا يَدْعُونَ مَعَ اللَّهِ إِلَٰهًا آخَرَ وَلَا يَقْتُلُونَ النَّفْسَ الَّتِي حَرَّمَ اللَّهُ إِلَّا بِالْحَقِّ وَلَا يَزْنُونَ ۚ وَمَنْ يَفْعَلْ ذَٰلِكَ يَلْقَ أَثَامًا ﴿٦٨﴾ ﴿الفرقان﴾

The servants of the Compassionate are the ones who walk humbly upon the earth, and when the foolish address them they say; "Peace" (63) and who spend the night before their Lord, prostrating and standing (in prayer) (64) and who say, "Our Lord! Avert from us the punishment of Hell! Truly its punishment is on-going (65) Verily, it is an evil abode and station" (66) and who, when they spend, are neither wasteful nor niggardly – and between those is a just balance (67) and who never invoke another deity with God nor take a life that God has forbidden save in (the pursuit of) justice, nor commit adultery and whoever does that shall meet retribution (68)

Al-Furqān (The Distinguisher) 25:63-68

إِلَّا مَنْ تَابَ وَآمَنَ وَعَمِلَ عَمَلًا صَالِحًا فَأُولَئِكَ يُبَدِّلُ اللَّهُ سَيِّئَاتِهِمْ حَسَنَاتٍ ۚ وَكَانَ اللَّهُ غَفُورًا رَحِيمًا ﴿٧٠﴾ وَمَنْ تَابَ وَعَمِلَ صَالِحًا فَإِنَّهُ يَتُوبُ إِلَى اللَّهِ مَتَابًا ﴿٧١﴾ وَالَّذِينَ لَا يَشْهَدُونَ الزُّورَ وَإِذَا مَرُّوا بِاللَّغْوِ مَرُّوا كِرَامًا ﴿٧٢﴾ وَالَّذِينَ إِذَا ذُكِّرُوا بِآيَاتِ رَبِّهِمْ لَمْ يَخِرُّوا عَلَيْهَا صُمًّا وَعُمْيَانًا ﴿٧٣﴾ وَالَّذِينَ يَقُولُونَ رَبَّنَا هَبْ لَنَا مِنْ أَزْوَاجِنَا وَذُرِّيَّاتِنَا قُرَّةَ أَعْيُنٍ وَاجْعَلْنَا لِلْمُتَّقِينَ إِمَامًا ﴿٧٤﴾ أُولَئِكَ يُجْزَوْنَ الْغُرْفَةَ بِمَا صَبَرُوا وَيُلَقَّوْنَ فِيهَا تَحِيَّةً وَسَلَامًا ﴿٧٥﴾ خَالِدِينَ فِيهَا ۚ حَسُنَتْ مُسْتَقَرًّا وَمُقَامًا ﴿٧٦﴾ ﴿الفرقان﴾

Save those who repent and believe and perform righteous deeds, for them, God will replace their evil deeds with good deeds. God is Forgiving, Merciful (70) And whoever has repented and performed righteous deeds, repents to God with true repentance (71) and those who never bear witness to what is false, and whenever they pass by (people engaged in) frivolity, pass by with dignity (72) and who, when they are reminded of signs of their Lord, fall not deaf and blind to them (73) and those who say, "Our Lord! Grant us comfort in our spouses and our offspring, and make us *imams* (good examples) for the God-conscious" (74) It is they who shall be rewarded with a high station (in Paradise) for their patience, and they shall be met therein with a greeting (of welcome) and peace (75) abiding therein. What a beautiful abode and resting place (76)

Al-Furqān (The Distinguisher) 25:70-76

الَّذِي خَلَقَنِي فَهُوَ يَهْدِينِ ﴿٧٨﴾ وَالَّذِي هُوَ يُطْعِمُنِي وَيَسْقِينِ ﴿٧٩﴾ وَإِذَا

مَرِضْتُ فَهُوَ يَشْفِينِ ﴿٨٠﴾ وَالَّذِي يُمِيتُنِي ثُمَّ يُحْيِينِ ﴿٨١﴾ وَالَّذِي أَطْمَعُ

أَنْ يَغْفِرَ لِي خَطِيئَتِي يَوْمَ الدِّينِ ﴿٨٢﴾ رَبِّ هَبْ لِي حُكْمًا وَأَلْحِقْنِي

بِالصَّالِحِينَ ﴿٨٣﴾ وَاجْعَلْ لِي لِسَانَ صِدْقٍ فِي الْآخِرِينَ ﴿٨٤﴾ وَاجْعَلْنِي

مِنْ وَرَثَةِ جَنَّةِ النَّعِيمِ ﴿٨٥﴾ وَاغْفِرْ لِأَبِي إِنَّهُ كَانَ مِنَ الضَّالِّينَ ﴿٨٦﴾ وَلَا

تُخْزِنِي يَوْمَ يُبْعَثُونَ ﴿٨٧﴾ يَوْمَ لَا يَنْفَعُ مَالٌ وَلَا بَنُونَ ﴿٨٨﴾ إِلَّا مَنْ أَتَى

اللَّهَ بِقَلْبٍ سَلِيمٍ ﴿٨٩﴾ وَأُزْلِفَتِ الْجَنَّةُ لِلْمُتَّقِينَ ﴿٩٠﴾ الشعراء﴾

Who created me, it is He who guides me (78) and the One Who gives
me food and drink (79) and when I am ill, He cures me (80) and the One
Who will cause me to die, then give me life (again) (81) and the One
Who, I hope, will forgive me my faults on the Day of Judgement (82)
My Lord! Grant me wisdom, and unite me with the righteous (83) and
grant me the power to convey the truth to later generations (84) and
make me among the inheritors of the Garden of bliss (85) and forgive
my father – for he is among those who have gone astray (86) and do
not disgrace me on the Day they are resurrected (87) the Day when
neither wealth nor children avail (88) save the one who comes before
God with a sound heart (89) And paradise will be brought near to the
God-conscious (90)

Al-Shu'araa (The Poets) 26:78-90

فَأَمَّا الَّذِينَ آمَنُوا وَعَمِلُوا الصَّالِحَاتِ فَهُمْ فِي رَوْضَةٍ يُحْبَرُونَ ﴿١٥﴾

﴿الروم﴾

As for those who believe and perform righteous deeds, they will delight in a Garden (15)

Al-Rūm (The Byzantines) 30:15

فَسُبْحَانَ اللَّهِ حِينَ تُمْسُونَ وَحِينَ تُصْبِحُونَ ﴿١٧﴾ ﴿الروم﴾

So give glory to God when you reach the evening and when you rise in the morning (17)

Al-Rūm (The Byzantines) 30:17

وَلَهُ الحَمدُ فِي السَّماواتِ وَالأَرضِ وَعَشِيًّا وَحينَ تُظهِرونَ ﴿١٨﴾ ﴿الروم﴾

And all praise belongs to Him in the heavens and the earth; and in the late afternoon and at noon (18)

Al-Rūm (The Byzantines) 30:18

وَمِن آيَاتِهِ أَن خَلَقَكُم مِن تُرَابٍ ثُمَّ إِذَا أَنتُم بَشَرٌ تَنتَشِرُونَ ﴿٢٠﴾ ﴿الروم﴾

And among His signs is that He created you from dust, and behold you are human beings scattered (far and wide) (20)

Al-Rūm (The Byzantines) 30:20

وَمِن آيَاتِهِ أَن خَلَقَ لَكُم مِن أَنفُسِكُم أَزواجًا لِتَسكُنوا إِلَيها وَجَعَلَ بَينَكُم

مَوَدَّةً وَرَحمَةً ۚ إِنَّ فِي ذَٰلِكَ لَآيَاتٍ لِقَومٍ يَتَفَكَّرونَ ﴿21﴾ ﴿الروم﴾

And among His signs is that He created for you mates from among
yourselves, that you may dwell with in love and mercy. Surely in that
are signs for a people who reflect (21)

Al-Rūm (The Byzantines) 30:21

وَمِن آيَاتِهِ خَلْقُ السَّماوَاتِ وَالأَرضِ وَاختِلافُ أَلسِنَتِكُم وَأَلوانِكُم ۚ إِنَّ في

ذٰلِكَ لَآياتٍ لِلعالِمِينَ ﴿٢٢﴾ ﴿الروم﴾

And among His signs is the creation of the heavens and the earth, and the variations of your languages and colours. Surely in that are signs for those who know (22)

Al-Rūm (The Byzantines) 30:22

وَمِن آيَاتِهِ مَنامُكُم بِاللَّيلِ وَالنَّهارِ وَابتِغاؤُكُم مِن فَضلِهِ ۚ إِنَّ في ذٰلِكَ لَآيَاتٍ لِقَومٍ يَسمَعونَ ﴿٢٣﴾ ﴿الروم﴾

And among His signs is your sleep, by night and by day, and your quest of His Bounty. Surely in this are signs for a people who listen (23)

Al-Rūm (The Byzantines) 30:23

وَمِن آياتِهِ يُريكُمُ البَرقَ خَوفًا وَطَمَعًا وَيُنَزِّلُ مِنَ السَّماءِ ماءً فَيُحيي بِهِ الأَرضَ بَعدَ مَوتِها ۚ إِنَّ في ذٰلِكَ لَآياتٍ لِقَومٍ يَعقِلونَ ﴿٢٤﴾ ﴿الروم﴾

And among His signs, He shows you the lightning to give fear and hope and He sends down water from the sky thereby reviving the earth after death. Surely in this are signs for a people who use their intellect (24)

Al-Rūm (The Byzantines) 30:24

وَمِن آيَاتِهِ أَن تَقومَ السَّماءُ وَالأَرضُ بِأَمرِهِ ثُمَّ إِذا دَعاكُم دَعوَةً مِنَ الأَرضِ
إِذا أَنتُم تَخرُجونَ ﴿٢٥﴾ ﴿الروم﴾

And among His signs, that heaven and earth stand by His Command,
then when He calls you with a single call; behold from the earth you
will emerge (25)

Al-Rūm (The Byzantines) 30:25

وَلَهُ مَن فِي السَّمَاوَاتِ وَالأَرْضِ ۖ كُلٌّ لَهُ قَانِتُونَ ﴿٢٦﴾ ﴿الروم﴾

Unto Him belongs every being that is in the heavens and on the earth: all are obedient to Him (26)

Al-Rūm (The Byzantines) 30:26

وَهُوَ الَّذِي يَبْدَأُ الخَلقَ ثُمَّ يُعِيدُهُ وَهُوَ أَهوَنُ عَلَيهِ ، وَلَهُ المَثَلُ الأَعلىٰ فِي السَّماواتِ وَالأَرضِ ، وَهُوَ العَزيزُ الحَكيمُ ﴿٢٧﴾ ﴿الروم﴾

It is He Who begins creation then repeats it, and it is most easy for Him. His is the sublime similitude in the heavens and the earth. And He is the Almighty, the Wise (27)

Al-Rūm (The Byzantines) 30:27

فَأَقِمْ وَجْهَكَ لِلدِّينِ الْقَيِّمِ مِنْ قَبْلِ أَنْ يَأْتِيَ يَوْمٌ لَا مَرَدَّ لَهُ مِنَ اللَّهِ يَوْمَئِذٍ يَصَّدَّعُونَ ﴿٤٣﴾ ﴿الروم﴾

Set, thy face steadfast toward the upright religion, before a Day comes from God that cannot be averted. On that Day mankind will be divided (43)

Al-Rūm (The Byzantines) 30:43

وَمِنْ آيَاتِهِ أَنْ يُرْسِلَ الرِّيَاحَ مُبَشِّرَاتٍ وَلِيُذِيقَكُم مِنْ رَحْمَتِهِ وَلِتَجْرِيَ الْفُلْكُ بِأَمْرِهِ وَلِتَبْتَغُوا مِنْ فَضْلِهِ وَلَعَلَّكُمْ تَشْكُرُونَ ﴿٤٦﴾ ﴿الروم﴾

And among His signs is that He sends the winds as bearers of glad tidings to give you a taste of His Mercy, and that the ships may sail by His Command, and that you may seek His Grace, and that you may be grateful (46)

Al-Rūm (The Byzantines) 30:46

تِلْكَ آيَاتُ الْكِتَابِ الْحَكِيمِ ﴿٢﴾ هُدًى وَرَحْمَةً لِلْمُحْسِنِينَ ﴿٣﴾ الَّذِينَ يُقِيمُونَ الصَّلَاةَ وَيُؤْتُونَ الزَّكَاةَ وَهُم بِالْآخِرَةِ هُمْ يُوقِنُونَ ﴿٤﴾ أُولَٰئِكَ عَلَىٰ هُدًى مِّن رَّبِّهِمْ ۖ وَأُولَٰئِكَ هُمُ الْمُفْلِحُونَ ﴿٥﴾ ﴿لقمان﴾

These are revelations of the Wise Scripture (2) a guidance and a mercy for the virtuous (3) who are steadfast in prayer and give the alms and who are certain of the Hereafter (4) They are upon guidance from their Lord, and it is they who shall prosper (5)

Luqmān (Luqman) 31:2-5

إِنَّ الَّذِينَ آمَنُوا وَعَمِلُوا الصَّالِحَاتِ لَهُمْ جَنَّاتُ النَّعِيمِ ﴿٨﴾ خَالِدِينَ فِيهَا ۚ

وَعْدَ اللَّهِ حَقًّا ۚ وَهُوَ الْعَزِيزُ الْحَكِيمُ ﴿٩﴾ ﴿لقمان﴾

Truly those who believe and perform righteous deeds, theirs shall be
Gardens of bliss (8) Abiding therein – a promise of God in truth. And He
is the Almighty, the Wise (9)

Luqmān (Luqman) 31:8-9

يَا بُنَيَّ إِنَّهَا إِنْ تَكُ مِثْقَالَ حَبَّةٍ مِنْ خَرْدَلٍ فَتَكُنْ فِي صَخْرَةٍ أَوْ فِي السَّمَاوَاتِ أَوْ فِي الْأَرْضِ يَأْتِ بِهَا اللَّهُ ۚ إِنَّ اللَّهَ لَطِيفٌ خَبِيرٌ ﴿١٦﴾

﴿لقمان﴾

Oh my son! If it be but the weight of a grain of mustard seed, be it (hidden) in a rock, or in the heavens or on the earth, God will bring it forth. Truly God is Gracious, All-Aware (16)

Luqmān (Luqman) 31:16

وَمَنْ يُسْلِمْ وَجْهَهُ إِلَى اللَّهِ وَهُوَ مُحْسِنٌ فَقَدِ اسْتَمْسَكَ بِالْعُرْوَةِ الْوُثْقَى ۚ وَإِلَى

اللَّهِ عَاقِبَةُ الْأُمُورِ ﴿٢٢﴾ ﴿لقمان﴾

And whoever submits his face (himself) to God and is virtuous has indeed grasped the most trustworthy handhold, and unto God is the final outcome (of all things) (22)

Luqmān (Luqman) 31:22

مَا خَلْقُكُمْ وَلَا بَعْثُكُمْ إِلَّا كَنَفْسٍ وَاحِدَةٍ ۚ إِنَّ اللَّهَ سَمِيعٌ بَصِيرٌ ﴿٢٨﴾

﴿لقمان﴾

Your creation and your resurrection is but (like creating and resurrecting) a single soul. Truly God is Hearing, Seeing (28)

Luqmān (Luqman) 31:28

إِنَّ اللَّهَ عِنْدَهُ عِلْمُ السَّاعَةِ وَيُنَزِّلُ الْغَيْثَ وَيَعْلَمُ مَا فِي الْأَرْحَامِ ۖ وَمَا تَدْرِي نَفْسٌ مَاذَا تَكْسِبُ غَدًا ۖ وَمَا تَدْرِي نَفْسٌ بِأَيِّ أَرْضٍ تَمُوتُ ۚ إِنَّ اللَّهَ عَلِيمٌ خَبِيرٌ ﴿٣٤﴾ ﴿لقمان﴾

Truly with God rests the knowledge of the Hour and He sends down the rain and knows what is in the wombs. And no soul knows what it will reap tomorrow, and no soul knows in what land it will die. Truly God is All-Knowing, All-Aware (34)

Luqmān (Luqman) 31:34

فَلَا تَعْلَمُ نَفْسٌ مَا أُخْفِيَ لَهُمْ مِنْ قُرَّةِ أَعْيُنٍ جَزَاءً بِمَا كَانُوا يَعْمَلُونَ ﴿١٧﴾ أَفَمَنْ كَانَ مُؤْمِنًا كَمَنْ كَانَ فَاسِقًا ۚ لَا يَسْتَوُونَ ﴿١٨﴾ أَمَّا الَّذِينَ آمَنُوا وَعَمِلُوا الصَّالِحَاتِ فَلَهُمْ جَنَّاتُ الْمَأْوَىٰ نُزُلًا بِمَا كَانُوا يَعْمَلُونَ ﴿١٩﴾

﴿السجدة﴾

No soul knows what is kept hidden in store for them of blissful delights as a reward for all that they have done (17) Is one who believes like one who defies God? They are not equal (18) As for those who believe and perform righteous deeds, theirs shall be Gardens of refuge, as a welcome for all that they have done (19)

Al-Sajdah (The Prostration) 32:17-19

وَتَوَكَّلْ عَلَى اللَّهِ ۚ وَكَفَىٰ بِاللَّهِ وَكِيلًا ﴿٣﴾ ﴿الأحزاب﴾

And place thy trust in God; God suffices as a Guardian (3)

Al-Ahzāb (The Confederates) 33:3

لَقَدْ كَانَ لَكُمْ فِي رَسُولِ اللَّهِ أُسْوَةٌ حَسَنَةٌ لِمَنْ كَانَ يَرْجُو اللَّهَ وَالْيَوْمَ الْآخِرَ

وَذَكَرَ اللَّهَ كَثِيرًا ﴿٢١﴾ ﴿الأحزاب﴾

Indeed, you have in the Messenger of God a good example for anyone whose hope is in God and the Last Day, and remembers God much (21)

Al-Ahzāb (The Confederates) 33:21

إِنَّ الْمُسْلِمِينَ وَالْمُسْلِمَاتِ وَالْمُؤْمِنِينَ وَالْمُؤْمِنَاتِ وَالْقَانِتِينَ وَالْقَانِتَاتِ وَالصَّادِقِينَ وَالصَّادِقَاتِ وَالصَّابِرِينَ وَالصَّابِرَاتِ وَالْخَاشِعِينَ وَالْخَاشِعَاتِ وَالْمُتَصَدِّقِينَ وَالْمُتَصَدِّقَاتِ وَالصَّائِمِينَ وَالصَّائِمَاتِ وَالْحَافِظِينَ فُرُوجَهُمْ وَالْحَافِظَاتِ وَالذَّاكِرِينَ اللَّهَ كَثِيرًا وَالذَّاكِرَاتِ أَعَدَّ اللَّهُ لَهُم مَّغْفِرَةً وَأَجْرًا عَظِيمًا ﴿٣٥﴾ ﴿الأحزاب﴾

Verily for surrendering men and surrendering women, and believing men and believing women, devout men and devout women, truthful men and truthful and women, patient men and patient women, humble men and humble women, charitable men and charitable women, and men who fast and women who fast, and men who guard their modesty and women who guard (their modesty), and men who remember God much and women who remember, God has prepared for them forgiveness and a great reward (35)

Al-Ahzāb (The Confederates) 33:35

الَّذِينَ يُبَلِّغُونَ رِسَالاتِ اللَّهِ وَيَخْشَوْنَهُ وَلا يَخْشَوْنَ أَحَدًا إِلَّا اللَّهَ ۚ وَكَفَىٰ بِاللَّهِ حَسِيبًا ﴿٣٩﴾ ﴿الأحزاب﴾

Those who convey God's messages and are in awe of Him and are in awe of none but God and God's reckoning is enough (39)

Al-Ahzāb (The Confederates) 33:39

يَا أَيُّهَا الَّذِينَ آمَنُوا اذْكُرُوا اللَّهَ ذِكْرًا كَثِيرًا ﴿٤١﴾ وَسَبِّحُوهُ بُكْرَةً وَأَصِيلًا ﴿٤٢﴾ هُوَ الَّذِي يُصَلِّي عَلَيْكُمْ وَمَلَائِكَتُهُ لِيُخْرِجَكُمْ مِنَ الظُّلُمَاتِ إِلَى النُّورِ ۚ وَكَانَ بِالْمُؤْمِنِينَ رَحِيمًا ﴿٤٣﴾ ﴿الأحزاب﴾

O you who believe! Remember God with much remembrance (41) and glorify Him morning and evening (42) It is He who blesses you, as do His angels, that He may lead you out of the depths of darkness into the light. And He is Merciful unto the believers (43)

Al-Ahzāb (The Confederates) 33:41-43

يَا أَيُّهَا الَّذِينَ آمَنُوا اتَّقُوا اللَّهَ وَقُولُوا قَوْلًا سَدِيدًا ﴿٧٠﴾ يُصْلِحْ لَكُمْ أَعْمَالَكُمْ وَيَغْفِرْ لَكُمْ ذُنُوبَكُمْ ۗ وَمَنْ يُطِعِ اللَّهَ وَرَسُولَهُ فَقَدْ فَازَ فَوْزًا عَظِيمًا ﴿٧١﴾

﴿الأحزاب﴾

O you who believe! Be mindful of God and speak justly (70) that He may fix your deeds aright and forgive you your sins, and whoever obeys God and His Messenger has already achieved a great triumph (71)

Al-Ahzāb (The Confederates) 33:70-71

الْحَمْدُ لِلَّهِ الَّذِي لَهُ مَا فِي السَّمَاوَاتِ وَمَا فِي الْأَرْضِ وَلَهُ الْحَمْدُ فِي الْآخِرَةِ ۚ

وَهُوَ الْحَكِيمُ الْخَبِيرُ ﴿١﴾ يَعْلَمُ مَا يَلِجُ فِي الْأَرْضِ وَمَا يَخْرُجُ مِنْهَا وَمَا يَنْزِلُ

مِنَ السَّمَاءِ وَمَا يَعْرُجُ فِيهَا ۚ وَهُوَ الرَّحِيمُ الْغَفُورُ ﴿٢﴾ ﴿سبأ﴾

Praise be to God, unto Him belongs all that is in the heavens and all that is on the earth. His is the praise in the Hereafter, and He is the Wise, the All-Aware (1) He knows all that enters the earth and all that comes out of it, and all that descends from the Heavens and all that ascends to them. And He is the Merciful, the Forgiving (2)

Saba (Sheba) 34:1-2

لِيَجْزِيَ الَّذِينَ آمَنُوا وَعَمِلُوا الصَّالِحَاتِ ۚ أُولَٰئِكَ لَهُم مَّغْفِرَةٌ وَرِزْقٌ كَرِيمٌ ﴿٤﴾ ﴿سبأ﴾

That He may reward those who believe and perform righteous deeds; it is they who shall have forgiveness and a generous provision (4)

Saba (Sheba) 34:4

وَيَرَى الَّذِينَ أُوتُوا الْعِلْمَ الَّذِي أُنزِلَ إِلَيْكَ مِنْ رَبِّكَ هُوَ الْحَقَّ وَيَهْدِي إِلَىٰ صِرَاطِ الْعَزِيزِ الْحَمِيدِ ﴿٦﴾ ﴿سبأ﴾

Those who have been endowed with knowledge see that what has been sent down upon thee from thy Lord is indeed the truth and that it guides to the path of the Almighty, the Praised (6)

Saba (Sheba) 34:6

مَنْ كَانَ يُرِيدُ الْعِزَّةَ فَلِلَّهِ الْعِزَّةُ جَمِيعًا ۚ إِلَيْهِ يَصْعَدُ الْكَلِمُ الطَّيِّبُ وَالْعَمَلُ

الصَّالِحُ يَرْفَعُهُ ۚ وَالَّذِينَ يَمْكُرُونَ السَّيِّئَاتِ لَهُمْ عَذَابٌ شَدِيدٌ ۖ وَمَكْرُ أُولَٰئِكَ

هُوَ يَبُورُ ﴿١٠﴾ ﴿فاطر﴾

Whoever desires might – to God belongs all might. Unto Him all good words ascend, and the righteous deeds He raises. But for those who plot evil deeds, a severe punishment awaits them, and their plotting will come to naught (10)

Fātir (The Originator) 35:10

يَا أَيُّهَا النَّاسُ أَنْتُمُ الْفُقَرَاءُ إِلَى اللَّهِ ۖ وَاللَّهُ هُوَ الْغَنِيُّ الْحَمِيدُ ﴿١٥﴾ إِنْ يَشَأْ يُذْهِبْكُمْ وَيَأْتِ بِخَلْقٍ جَدِيدٍ ﴿١٦﴾ وَمَا ذَٰلِكَ عَلَى اللَّهِ بِعَزِيزٍ ﴿١٧﴾

﴿فاطر﴾

O mankind! It is you who are in need of God, and God is the Self-Sufficient, the Praised (15) If He wills, He could do away with you and bring forth a new creation (16) Nor is that difficult for God (17)

Fātir (The Originator) 35:15-17

وَلَا تَزِرُ وَازِرَةٌ وِزْرَ أُخْرَىٰ ۚ وَإِن تَدْعُ مُثْقَلَةٌ إِلَىٰ حِمْلِهَا لَا يُحْمَلْ مِنْهُ شَيْءٌ

وَلَوْ كَانَ ذَا قُرْبَىٰ ۗ إِنَّمَا تُنذِرُ الَّذِينَ يَخْشَوْنَ رَبَّهُم بِالْغَيْبِ وَأَقَامُوا الصَّلَاةَ ۚ

وَمَن تَزَكَّىٰ فَإِنَّمَا يَتَزَكَّىٰ لِنَفْسِهِ ۚ وَإِلَى اللَّهِ الْمَصِيرُ ﴿١٨﴾ ﴿فاطر﴾

And none shall bear the burden of another. And if one heavily bur-
dened (soul) calls for his burden to be borne, naught of it will be borne,
even if it be near of kin. You can warn only those who are in awe of
their Lord unseen and steadfast in prayer. And whoever purifies himself, purifies it for his own self. And unto God is the journey's end (18)

Fātir (The Originator) 35:18

وَمَا يَسْتَوِي الْأَعْمَىٰ وَالْبَصِيرُ ﴿١٩﴾ وَلَا الظُّلُمَاتُ وَلَا النُّورُ ﴿٢٠﴾ وَلَا الظِّلُّ وَلَا الْحَرُورُ ﴿٢١﴾ ﴿فاطر﴾

The blind and the seeing are not alike (19) nor are the depths of darkness and the light (20) nor the shade and the scorching heat (21)

Fātir (The Originator) 35:19-21

إِنَّ الَّذِينَ يَتْلُونَ كِتَابَ اللَّهِ وَأَقَامُوا الصَّلَاةَ وَأَنْفَقُوا مِمَّا رَزَقْنَاهُمْ سِرًّا وَعَلَانِيَةً يَرْجُونَ تِجَارَةً لَنْ تَبُورَ ﴿٢٩﴾ لِيُوَفِّيَهُمْ أُجُورَهُمْ وَيَزِيدَهُمْ مِنْ فَضْلِهِ ۚ إِنَّهُ غَفُورٌ شَكُورٌ ﴿٣٠﴾ ﴿فاطر﴾

Truly those who recite the Scripture of God, are steadfast in prayer and spend from what We have provided them secretly and openly may hope for a trade that will never cease (29) For He will pay them their rewards and increase them from His Bounty. Truly He is Forgiving, Thankful (30)

Fātir (The Originator) 35:29-30

سَلَامٌ قَوْلًا مِنْ رَبٍّ رَحِيمٍ ﴿٥٨﴾ ﴿يس﴾

"Peace!" A word from a Lord Most Merciful (58)

Yā Sīn (Ya Sin) 36:58

لَوْ أَرَادَ اللَّهُ أَنْ يَتَّخِذَ وَلَدًا لَاصْطَفَىٰ مِمَّا يَخْلُقُ مَا يَشَاءُ ۚ سُبْحَانَهُ ۖ هُوَ اللَّهُ الْوَاحِدُ الْقَهَّارُ ﴿٤﴾ ﴿الزمر﴾

Had God wished to take a child (for Himself), He could have chosen whom He pleased from what He created. Glory be to Him; He is God, the One, the Absolute (4)

Al-Zumar (The Throngs) 39:4

خَلَقَ السَّمَاوَاتِ وَالْأَرْضَ بِالْحَقِّ ۖ يُكَوِّرُ اللَّيْلَ عَلَى النَّهَارِ وَيُكَوِّرُ النَّهَارَ عَلَى اللَّيْلِ ۖ وَسَخَّرَ الشَّمْسَ وَالْقَمَرَ ۖ كُلٌّ يَجْرِي لِأَجَلٍ مُسَمًّى ۚ أَلَا هُوَ الْعَزِيزُ الْغَفَّارُ ﴿٥﴾ ﴿الزمر﴾

He created the heavens and the earth in truth. He wraps the night into the day and wraps the day into the night, and He made the sun and the moon subservient, each running for a specified time. Is He not the Almighty, the Forgiving? (5)

Al-Zumar (The Throngs) 39:5

أَمَّنْ هُوَ قَانِتٌ آنَاءَ اللَّيْلِ سَاجِدًا وَقَائِمًا يَحْذَرُ الْآخِرَةَ وَيَرْجُو رَحْمَةَ رَبِّهِۦ قُلْ هَلْ يَسْتَوِي الَّذِينَ يَعْلَمُونَ وَالَّذِينَ لَا يَعْلَمُونَۗ إِنَّمَا يَتَذَكَّرُ أُولُو الْأَلْبَابِ ﴿٩﴾ ﴿الزمر﴾

What of the one who worships devoutly during the night, prostrating and standing (in prayer), ever mindful of the Hereafter, hoping for the Mercy of his Lord? Say "Are those who know and those who do not know equal? Only those who possess intellect will remember" (9)

Al-Zumar (The Throngs) 39:9

قُلْ يَا عِبَادِ الَّذِينَ آمَنُوا اتَّقُوا رَبَّكُمْ ۚ لِلَّذِينَ أَحْسَنُوا فِي هٰذِهِ الدُّنْيَا حَسَنَةٌ ۗ وَأَرْضُ اللَّهِ وَاسِعَةٌ ۗ إِنَّمَا يُوَفَّى الصَّابِرُونَ أَجْرَهُمْ بِغَيْرِ حِسَابٍ ﴿١٠﴾

﴿الزمر﴾

Say, "O My servants who believe, be conscious of your Lord. For those who do good in this world there is good, and God's earth is wide." Surely those who are patient shall receive their reward in full without reckoning (10)

Al-Zumar (The Throngs) 39:10

لٰكِنِ الَّذِينَ اتَّقَوْا رَبَّهُمْ لَهُمْ غُرَفٌ مِنْ فَوْقِهَا غُرَفٌ مَبْنِيَّةٌ تَجْرِي مِنْ تَحْتِهَا الْأَنْهَارُ ۖ وَعْدَ اللَّهِ ۖ لَا يُخْلِفُ اللَّهُ الْمِيعَادَ ﴿٢٠﴾ ﴿الزمر﴾

But as for those who are mindful of their Lord, they will have lofty dwellings built one above the other, beneath which rivers flow. This is God's promise; God never fails to fulfil His promise (20)

Al-Zumar (The Throngs) 39:20

أَفَمَنْ شَرَحَ اللَّهُ صَدْرَهُ لِلْإِسْلَامِ فَهُوَ عَلَىٰ نُورٍ مِنْ رَبِّهِ ۚ فَوَيْلٌ لِلْقَاسِيَةِ قُلُوبُهُمْ مِنْ ذِكْرِ اللَّهِ ۚ أُولَٰئِكَ فِي ضَلَالٍ مُبِينٍ ﴿٢٢﴾ ﴿الزمر﴾

Is one whose heart God has opened to submission, so that he follows a light from his Lord (no better than the hard-hearted?) Woe unto those whose hearts are hardened from the remembrance of God! They are clearly in error (22)

Al-Zumar (The Throngs) 39:22

اللَّهُ نَزَّلَ أَحْسَنَ الْحَدِيثِ كِتَابًا مُتَشَابِهًا مَثَانِيَ تَقْشَعِرُّ مِنْهُ جُلُودُ الَّذِينَ يَخْشَوْنَ رَبَّهُمْ ثُمَّ تَلِينُ جُلُودُهُمْ وَقُلُوبُهُمْ إِلَىٰ ذِكْرِ اللَّهِ ۚ ذَٰلِكَ هُدَى اللَّهِ يَهْدِي بِهِ مَنْ يَشَاءُ ۚ وَمَنْ يُضْلِلِ اللَّهُ فَمَا لَهُ مِنْ هَادٍ ﴿٢٣﴾ ﴿الزمر﴾

God has sent down the most beautiful teachings, a Scripture consistent within itself, repeating (its teachings in truth), whereat quiver the skins of those who are in awe of their Lord. Then their skin and their hearts soften at the remembrance of God. Such is God's guidance; He guides whomever He will and whomever God leads astray, no guide has he (23)

Al-Zumar (The Throngs) 39:23

قُل يَا عِبَادِيَ الَّذِينَ أَسْرَفُوا عَلَىٰ أَنْفُسِهِمْ لَا تَقْنَطُوا مِنْ رَحْمَةِ اللَّهِ ۚ إِنَّ اللَّهَ
يَغْفِرُ الذُّنُوبَ جَمِيعًا ۚ إِنَّهُ هُوَ الْغَفُورُ الرَّحِيمُ ﴿٥٣﴾ ﴿الزمر﴾

Say, "O My servants who have transgressed against your own selves! Do not despair of God's Mercy. Indeed, God forgives all sins. Truly He is the Forgiving, the Merciful (53)

Al-Zumar (The Throngs) 39:53

وَيُنَجِّي اللَّهُ الَّذِينَ اتَّقَوْا بِمَفَازَتِهِمْ لَا يَمَسُّهُمُ السُّوءُ وَلَا هُمْ يَحْزَنُونَ ﴿٦١﴾ اللَّهُ خَالِقُ كُلِّ شَيْءٍ ۖ وَهُوَ عَلَىٰ كُلِّ شَيْءٍ وَكِيلٌ ﴿٦٢﴾ ﴿الزمر﴾

And God safeguards those who were mindful (of Him) by virtue of their triumph; no evil shall touch them; nor shall they grieve (61) God is the Creator of all things, and He is Guardian over all things (62)

Al-Zumar (The Throngs) 39:61-62

وَسِيقَ الَّذِينَ اتَّقَوْا رَبَّهُمْ إِلَى الْجَنَّةِ زُمَرًا ۔ حَتَّىٰ إِذَا جَاءُوهَا وَفُتِحَتْ أَبْوَابُهَا وَقَالَ لَهُمْ خَزَنَتُهَا سَلَامٌ عَلَيْكُمْ طِبْتُمْ فَادْخُلُوهَا خَالِدِينَ ﴿٧٣﴾ وَقَالُوا الْحَمْدُ لِلَّهِ الَّذِي صَدَقَنَا وَعْدَهُ وَأَوْرَثَنَا الْأَرْضَ نَتَبَوَّأُ مِنَ الْجَنَّةِ حَيْثُ نَشَاءُ ۔ فَنِعْمَ أَجْرُ الْعَامِلِينَ ﴿٧٤﴾ وَتَرَى الْمَلَائِكَةَ حَافِّينَ مِنْ حَوْلِ الْعَرْشِ يُسَبِّحُونَ بِحَمْدِ رَبِّهِمْ ۔ وَقُضِيَ بَيْنَهُمْ بِالْحَقِّ وَقِيلَ الْحَمْدُ لِلَّهِ رَبِّ الْعَالَمِينَ ﴿٧٥﴾ ﴿الزمر﴾

Those who are mindful of their Lord will be led in throngs to paradise. When they reach it, its gates will be opened, and its keepers will say unto them "Peace be upon you! You have been good, so enter it to abide therein" (73) and they will say "Praise be to God who has kept His promise to us and has made us inherit this land, that we may settle in paradise wherever we please" How excellent is the reward for those who laboured! (74) And you shall see the angels surrounding the Throne, glorifying the praise of their Lord. Judgement shall be made between them in truth, and it will be said, "Praise be to God, Lord of the Worlds" (75)

Al-Zumar (The Throngs) 39:73-75

الَّذِينَ يَحْمِلُونَ الْعَرْشَ وَمَنْ حَوْلَهُ يُسَبِّحُونَ بِحَمْدِ رَبِّهِمْ وَيُؤْمِنُونَ بِهِ وَيَسْتَغْفِرُونَ لِلَّذِينَ آمَنُوا رَبَّنَا وَسِعْتَ كُلَّ شَيْءٍ رَحْمَةً وَعِلْمًا فَاغْفِرْ لِلَّذِينَ تَابُوا وَاتَّبَعُوا سَبِيلَكَ وَقِهِمْ عَذَابَ الْجَحِيمِ ﴿٧﴾ رَبَّنَا وَأَدْخِلْهُمْ جَنَّاتِ عَدْنٍ الَّتِي وَعَدْتَهُمْ وَمَنْ صَلَحَ مِنْ آبَائِهِمْ وَأَزْوَاجِهِمْ وَذُرِّيَّاتِهِمْ ۚ إِنَّكَ أَنْتَ الْعَزِيزُ الْحَكِيمُ ﴿٨﴾ وَقِهِمُ السَّيِّئَاتِ ۚ وَمَنْ تَقِ السَّيِّئَاتِ يَوْمَئِذٍ فَقَدْ رَحِمْتَهُ ۚ وَذَٰلِكَ هُوَ الْفَوْزُ الْعَظِيمُ ﴿٩﴾ ﴿غافر﴾

Those who bear the Throne and who are around it, glorify the praise of their Lord and believe in Him and seek forgiveness for those who believe; "Our Lord, Thou embracest all things in Mercy and Knowledge. Forgive those who repent and follow Thy path, and shield them from the torment of the Blaze (7) Our Lord, and grant them entry to the Gardens of Eden which Thou hast promised them, together with the righteous among their fathers, their spouses and their descendants. Truly Thou art the Almighty, the Wise (8) And protect them from evil deeds, whoever You shield from evil deeds on that Day will receive Your mercy. And that is the supreme triumph" (9)

Ghāfir (The Forgiver) 40:7-9

مَنْ عَمِلَ سَيِّئَةً فَلَا يُجْزَىٰ إِلَّا مِثْلَهَا ۖ وَمَنْ عَمِلَ صَالِحًا مِنْ ذَكَرٍ أَوْ أُنْثَىٰ

وَهُوَ مُؤْمِنٌ فَأُولَٰئِكَ يَدْخُلُونَ الْجَنَّةَ يُرْزَقُونَ فِيهَا بِغَيْرِ حِسَابٍ ﴿٤٠﴾

﴿غافر﴾

Whoever does an evil deed will be requited with its like and whoever does a righteous deed from men or women and is a believer shall enter paradise wherein they will be provided for without reckoning (40)

Ghāfir (The Forgiver) 40:40

اللَّهُ الَّذِي جَعَلَ لَكُمُ الْأَرْضَ قَرَارًا وَالسَّمَاءَ بِنَاءً وَصَوَّرَكُمْ فَأَحْسَنَ صُوَرَكُمْ

وَرَزَقَكُم مِنَ الطَّيِّبَاتِ ۚ ذَٰلِكُمُ اللَّهُ رَبُّكُمْ ـ فَتَبَارَكَ اللَّهُ رَبُّ الْعَالَمِينَ ﴿٦٤﴾

هُوَ الْحَيُّ لَا إِلَٰهَ إِلَّا هُوَ فَادْعُوهُ مُخْلِصِينَ لَهُ الدِّينَ ۚ الْحَمْدُ لِلَّهِ رَبِّ الْعَالَمِينَ

﴿٦٥﴾ ﴿غافر﴾

It is God who made the earth a resting place for you and the sky a canopy. And He Who formed you and perfected your forms, and provided you with good things. That is God, your Lord; so blessed is God, Lord of the Worlds (64) He is the Ever-Living; there is no god but He. So call upon Him, in sincere religion to Him. Praise be to God, Lord of the Worlds (65)

Ghāfir (The Forgiver) 40:64-65

إِنَّ الَّذِينَ قَالُوا رَبُّنَا اللَّهُ ثُمَّ اسْتَقَامُوا تَتَنَزَّلُ عَلَيْهِمُ الْمَلَائِكَةُ أَلَّا تَخَافُوا

وَلَا تَحْزَنُوا وَأَبْشِرُوا بِالْجَنَّةِ الَّتِي كُنْتُمْ تُوعَدُونَ ﴿٣٠﴾ نَحْنُ أَوْلِيَاؤُكُمْ فِي

الْحَيَاةِ الدُّنْيَا وَفِي الْآخِرَةِ ۖ وَلَكُمْ فِيهَا مَا تَشْتَهِي أَنْفُسُكُمْ وَلَكُمْ فِيهَا مَا

تَدَّعُونَ ﴿٣١﴾ نُزُلًا مِنْ غَفُورٍ رَحِيمٍ ﴿٣٢﴾ ﴿فصلت﴾

Truly those who say, "Our Lord is God," then stand firm, the angels will descend upon them, (saying), "Fear not, nor grieve, but receive glad tidings of the paradise that you have been promised (30) We are your guardians in the life of this world and in the Hereafter; therein you shall have all that your souls desire, and therein you shall have all that you ask for (31) A welcoming (gift) from the Most Forgiving, Most Merciful One" (32)

Fussilat (Elaborated) 41:30-32

وَمَنْ أَحْسَنُ قَوْلًا مِمَّنْ دَعَا إِلَى اللَّهِ وَعَمِلَ صَالِحًا وَقَالَ إِنَّنِي مِنَ الْمُسْلِمِينَ
﴿٣٣﴾ ﴿فصلت﴾

And who is better in speech than one who calls unto God, performs righteous deeds, and says, "Truly I am among those who surrender?" (33)

Fussilat (Elaborated) 41:33

وَلَا تَسْتَوِي الْحَسَنَةُ وَلَا السَّيِّئَةُ ۚ ادْفَعْ بِالَّتِي هِيَ أَحْسَنُ فَإِذَا الَّذِي بَيْنَكَ

وَبَيْنَهُ عَدَاوَةٌ كَأَنَّهُ وَلِيٌّ حَمِيمٌ ﴿٣٤﴾ وَمَا يُلَقَّاهَا إِلَّا الَّذِينَ صَبَرُوا وَمَا يُلَقَّاهَا

إِلَّا ذُو حَظٍّ عَظِيمٍ ﴿٣٥﴾ ﴿فصلت﴾

Nor can goodness and evil be equal. Repel (evil) with one which is better; then behold, the one between whom and thee was enmity will become as if he were a close, true friend (34) Yet none shall attain it save those who are patient, and none shall attain it save the possessors of great fortune (35)

Fussilat (Elaborated) 41:34-35

لَهُ مَا فِي السَّمَاوَاتِ وَمَا فِي الْأَرْضِ ۔ وَهُوَ الْعَلِيُّ الْعَظِيمُ ﴿٤﴾ تَكَادُ
السَّمَاوَاتُ يَتَفَطَّرْنَ مِنْ فَوْقِهِنَّ ۚ وَالْمَلَائِكَةُ يُسَبِّحُونَ بِحَمْدِ رَبِّهِمْ وَيَسْتَغْفِرُونَ
لِمَنْ فِي الْأَرْضِ ۗ أَلَا إِنَّ اللَّهَ هُوَ الْغَفُورُ الرَّحِيمُ ﴿٥﴾ ﴿الشورى﴾

Unto Him belongs all that is in the heavens and all that is on the earth and He is the Exalted, the Tremendous (4) The heavens are almost broken apart from above, while the angels glorify the praise of their Lord and seek forgiveness for those on earth. Lo! Truly God is the Forgiving, the Merciful (5)

Al-Shūrā (Consultation) 42:4-5

وَمَا اخْتَلَفْتُمْ فِيهِ مِنْ شَيْءٍ فَحُكْمُهُ إِلَى اللَّهِ ۚ ذَٰلِكُمُ اللَّهُ رَبِّي عَلَيْهِ تَوَكَّلْتُ وَإِلَيْهِ أُنِيبُ ﴿١٠﴾ ﴿الشورى﴾

And in whatever you differ, the verdict thereof rests with God. That is God, my Lord. In Him I put my trust and to Him I turn (10)

Al-Shūrā (Consultation) 42:10

فَلِذَلِكَ فَادْعُ ـ وَاسْتَقِمْ كَمَا أُمِرْتَ ـ وَلَا تَتَّبِعْ أَهْوَاءَهُمْ ـ وَقُلْ آمَنْتُ بِمَا أَنْزَلَ اللَّهُ مِنْ كِتَابٍ ـ وَأُمِرْتُ لِأَعْدِلَ بَيْنَكُمُ ـ اللَّهُ رَبُّنَا وَرَبُّكُمْ ـ لَنَا أَعْمَالُنَا وَلَكُمْ أَعْمَالُكُمْ ـ لَا حُجَّةَ بَيْنَنَا وَبَيْنَكُمُ ـ اللَّهُ يَجْمَعُ بَيْنَنَا ـ وَإِلَيْهِ الْمَصِيرُ ﴿١٥﴾

﴿الشورى﴾

Therefore, call (them to faith), and stand steadfast as thou hast been commanded. Follow not their desires, but say, "I believe in whatever Scripture God has sent down, and I am commanded to judge justly between you. God is our Lord and your Lord. To us our deeds, and to you your deeds. There is no contention between us and you. God will gather us together and unto Him is the journey's end" (15)

Al-Shūrā (Consultation) 42:15

اللّهُ لَطِيفٌ بِعِبَادِهِ يَرْزُقُ مَنْ يَشَاءُ ۖ وَهُوَ الْقَوِيُّ الْعَزِيزُ ﴿١٩﴾ ﴿الشورى﴾

God is gracious unto His servants; He provides (sustenance) for whomever He will, and He is the Powerful, the Almighty (19)

Al-Shūrā (Consultation) 42:19

تَرَى الظَّالِمِينَ مُشْفِقِينَ مِمَّا كَسَبُوا وَهُوَ وَاقِعٌ بِهِمْ ۚ وَالَّذِينَ آمَنُوا وَعَمِلُوا
الصَّالِحَاتِ فِي رَوْضَاتِ الْجَنَّاتِ ۖ لَهُم مَّا يَشَاءُونَ عِندَ رَبِّهِمْ ۚ ذَٰلِكَ هُوَ
الْفَضْلُ الْكَبِيرُ ﴿٢٢﴾ ذَٰلِكَ الَّذِي يُبَشِّرُ اللَّهُ عِبَادَهُ الَّذِينَ آمَنُوا وَعَمِلُوا
الصَّالِحَاتِ ۗ قُل لَّا أَسْأَلُكُمْ عَلَيْهِ أَجْرًا إِلَّا الْمَوَدَّةَ فِي الْقُرْبَىٰ ۗ وَمَن يَقْتَرِفْ
حَسَنَةً نَّزِدْ لَهُ فِيهَا حُسْنًا ۚ إِنَّ اللَّهَ غَفُورٌ شَكُورٌ ﴿٢٣﴾ ﴿الشورى﴾

Thou seest the wrongdoers fearful of what they have earned, and it will surely fall upon them. And those who believe and perform righteous deeds shall be in flowering meadows of the Gardens (of Paradise). They shall have whatever they desire from their Lord. That is the great bounty (22) It is of this that God gives glad tidings to His servants who believe and perform righteous deeds. Say, "No reward do I ask of you, save affection among kinsfolk." And whoever does a good deed, We shall increase it for him in goodness. Truly God is Forgiving, Thankful (23)

Al-Shūrā (Consultation) 42:22-23

وَهُوَ الَّذِي يَقْبَلُ التَّوْبَةَ عَنْ عِبَادِهِ وَيَعْفُو عَنِ السَّيِّئَاتِ وَيَعْلَمُ مَا تَفْعَلُونَ

﴿٢٥﴾ ﴿الشورى﴾

It is He Who accepts repentance from His servants and pardons evil deeds, and knows all that you do (25)

Al-Shūrā (Consultation) 42:25

وَهُوَ الَّذِي يُنَزِّلُ الغَيثَ مِن بَعدِ ما قَنَطوا وَيَنشُرُ رَحمَتَهُ ۚ وَهُوَ الوَلِيُّ الحَمِيدُ ﴿٢٨﴾ ﴿الشورى﴾

It is He Who sends down the rain after they have lost hope and spreads His mercy (far and wide). He is the Protector, Worthy of All Praise (28)

Al-Shūrā (Consultation) 42:28

وَمَآ أَصَٰبَكُم مِّن مُّصِيبَةٍ فَبِمَا كَسَبَتْ أَيْدِيكُمْ وَيَعْفُواْ عَن كَثِيرٍ ﴿٣٠﴾

﴿الشورى﴾

Whatever calamity befalls you, it is because of what your own hands have earned; and He pardons much (30)

Al-Shūrā (Consultation) 42:30

فَمَا أُوتِيتُمْ مِنْ شَيْءٍ فَمَتَاعُ الْحَيَاةِ الدُّنْيَا ۖ وَمَا عِنْدَ اللَّهِ خَيْرٌ وَأَبْقَىٰ لِلَّذِينَ آمَنُوا وَعَلَىٰ رَبِّهِمْ يَتَوَكَّلُونَ ﴿٣٦﴾ وَالَّذِينَ يَجْتَنِبُونَ كَبَائِرَ الْإِثْمِ وَالْفَوَاحِشَ وَإِذَا مَا غَضِبُوا هُمْ يَغْفِرُونَ ﴿٣٧﴾ وَالَّذِينَ اسْتَجَابُوا لِرَبِّهِمْ وَأَقَامُوا الصَّلَاةَ وَأَمْرُهُمْ شُورَىٰ بَيْنَهُمْ وَمِمَّا رَزَقْنَاهُمْ يُنْفِقُونَ ﴿٣٨﴾ وَالَّذِينَ إِذَا أَصَابَهُمُ الْبَغْيُ هُمْ يَنْتَصِرُونَ ﴿٣٩﴾ وَجَزَاءُ سَيِّئَةٍ مِثْلُهَا ۖ فَمَنْ عَفَا وَأَصْلَحَ فَأَجْرُهُ عَلَى اللَّهِ ۚ إِنَّهُ لَا يُحِبُّ الظَّالِمِينَ ﴿٤٠﴾ ﴿الشورى﴾

Whatever you have been given, is only for the (passing) enjoyment of the life of this world, but that which is with God is better and more enduring for those who believe and trust in their Lord (36) And those who avoid great sins and indecencies and who when they are angry, (even then) they forgive (37) And those who respond to their Lord and are steadfast in prayer, and their affairs a matter of consultation among them and spend from what We provided for them (38) And who when great wrong afflicts them, they defend themselves (39) And the requital of an evil is an evil like it. But whoever pardons and sets matters aright, his reward rests with God. Truly He does not love the wrongdoers (40)

Al-Shūrā (Consultation) 42:36-40

وَلَمَنْ صَبَرَ وَغَفَرَ إِنَّ ذَٰلِكَ لَمِنْ عَزْمِ الْأُمُورِ ﴿٤٣﴾ ﴿الشورى﴾

Indeed if one is patient and forgives, verily, this truly is one of the greatest things (43)

Al-Shūrā (Consultation) 42:43

صِرَاطِ اللَّهِ الَّذِي لَهُ مَا فِي السَّمَاوَاتِ وَمَا فِي الْأَرْضِ ۗ أَلَا إِلَى اللَّهِ تَصِيرُ الْأُمُورُ ﴿٥٣﴾ ﴿الشورى﴾

The path of God, unto Whom belongs all that is in the heavens and all that is on the earth. Truly, all matters journey unto God (53)

Al-Shūrā (Consultation) 42:53

يَا عِبَادِ لَا خَوْفٌ عَلَيْكُمُ الْيَوْمَ وَلَا أَنْتُمْ تَحْزَنُونَ ﴿٦٨﴾ الَّذِينَ آمَنُوا بِآيَاتِنَا وَكَانُوا مُسْلِمِينَ ﴿٦٩﴾ ادْخُلُوا الْجَنَّةَ أَنْتُمْ وَأَزْوَاجُكُمْ تُحْبَرُونَ ﴿٧٠﴾ يُطَافُ عَلَيْهِمْ بِصِحَافٍ مِنْ ذَهَبٍ وَأَكْوَابٍ ۖ وَفِيهَا مَا تَشْتَهِيهِ الْأَنْفُسُ وَتَلَذُّ الْأَعْيُنُ ۖ وَأَنْتُمْ فِيهَا خَالِدُونَ ﴿٧١﴾ وَتِلْكَ الْجَنَّةُ الَّتِي أُورِثْتُمُوهَا بِمَا كُنْتُمْ تَعْمَلُونَ ﴿٧٢﴾ لَكُمْ فِيهَا فَاكِهَةٌ كَثِيرَةٌ مِنْهَا تَأْكُلُونَ ﴿٧٣﴾ ﴿الزخرف﴾

O My servants! No fear is upon you this Day, nor shall you grieve (68)
Those who believed in Our revelations and have surrendered (69) Enter
Paradise you and your spouses with joy (70) Brought round them are
trays and goblets of gold, and therein is all that their souls desire and
their eyes delight. And therein you shall abide (71) This is the Garden
that you have been given for what you used to do (72) Therein for you
is abundant fruit for you to eat (73)

Al-Zukhruf (Ornaments of Gold) 43:68-73

318

إِنَّا أَنْزَلْنَاهُ فِي لَيْلَةٍ مُبَارَكَةٍ ۚ إِنَّا كُنَّا مُنْذِرِينَ ﴿٣﴾ فِيهَا يُفْرَقُ كُلُّ أَمْرٍ حَكِيمٍ ﴿٤﴾ أَمْرًا مِنْ عِنْدِنَا ۚ إِنَّا كُنَّا مُرْسِلِينَ ﴿٥﴾ رَحْمَةً مِنْ رَبِّكَ ۚ إِنَّهُ هُوَ السَّمِيعُ الْعَلِيمُ ﴿٦﴾ ﴿الدخان﴾

Truly We have sent it down on a blessed night – truly We are always warning (3) Wherein every wise command is made distinct (4) A command from Ourselves – truly We are always sending (messages of guidance) (5) A mercy from thy Lord, truly He is the All-Hearing, the All-Knowing (6)

Al-Dukhān (Smoke) 44:3-6

إِنَّ الْمُتَّقِينَ فِي مَقَامٍ أَمِينٍ ﴿٥١﴾ فِي جَنَّاتٍ وَعُيُونٍ ﴿٥٢﴾ يَلْبَسُونَ مِنْ سُنْدُسٍ وَإِسْتَبْرَقٍ مُتَقَابِلِينَ ﴿٥٣﴾ كَذَلِكَ وَزَوَّجْنَاهُمْ بِحُورٍ عِينٍ ﴿٥٤﴾ يَدْعُونَ فِيهَا بِكُلِّ فَاكِهَةٍ آمِنِينَ ﴿٥٥﴾ لَا يَذُوقُونَ فِيهَا الْمَوْتَ إِلَّا الْمَوْتَةَ الْأُولَىٰ ۖ وَوَقَاهُمْ عَذَابَ الْجَحِيمِ ﴿٥٦﴾ فَضْلًا مِنْ رَبِّكَ ۚ ذَٰلِكَ هُوَ الْفَوْزُ الْعَظِيمُ ﴿٥٧﴾ ﴿الدخان﴾

Truly the God-conscious are in a state of safety (51) Amid Gardens and Springs (52) Dressed in fine silk and rich brocade, facing one another (53) Thus it shall be. And We shall wed them to beautiful-eyed maidens (54) They call therein for every fruit in safety (55) They taste no death therein, save the first death. And He shielded them from the torment of the Blaze (56) A bounty from thy Lord. That is the supreme triumph (57)

Al-Dukhān (Smoke) 44:51-57

فَلِلَّهِ الْحَمْدُ رَبِّ السَّمَاوَاتِ وَرَبِّ الْأَرْضِ رَبِّ الْعَالَمِينَ ﴿٣٦﴾ وَلَهُ

الْكِبْرِيَاءُ فِي السَّمَاوَاتِ وَالْأَرْضِ ـ وَهُوَ الْعَزِيزُ الْحَكِيمُ ﴿٣٧﴾ ﴿الجاثية﴾

So praise be to God, Lord of the heavens and of the earth, Lord of the
Worlds (36) And His is the Majesty in the heavens and the earth, and He
is the Almighty, the Wise (37)

Al-Jāthiyah (Kneeling) 45:36-37

إِنَّ الَّذِينَ قَالُوا رَبُّنَا اللَّهُ ثُمَّ اسْتَقَامُوا فَلَا خَوْفٌ عَلَيْهِمْ وَلَا هُمْ يَحْزَنُونَ

﴿١٣﴾ أُولَٰئِكَ أَصْحَابُ الْجَنَّةِ خَالِدِينَ فِيهَا جَزَاءً بِمَا كَانُوا يَعْمَلُونَ ﴿١٤﴾

﴿الأحقاف﴾

Truly those who say, "Our Lord is God," then stand firm no fear shall come upon them nor shall they grieve (13) They are the inhabitants of paradise, abiding therein, a reward for what they used to do (14)

Al-Ahqāf (The Sand Dunes) 46:13-14

وَوَصَّيْنَا الْإِنْسَانَ بِوَالِدَيْهِ إِحْسَانًا ـ حَمَلَتْهُ أُمُّهُ كُرْهًا وَوَضَعَتْهُ كُرْهًا ـ وَحَمْلُهُ

وَفِصَالُهُ ثَلَاثُونَ شَهْرًا ـ حَتَّىٰ إِذَا بَلَغَ أَشُدَّهُ وَبَلَغَ أَرْبَعِينَ سَنَةً قَالَ رَبِّ

أَوْزِعْنِي أَنْ أَشْكُرَ نِعْمَتَكَ الَّتِي أَنْعَمْتَ عَلَيَّ وَعَلَىٰ وَالِدَيَّ وَأَنْ أَعْمَلَ

صَالِحًا تَرْضَاهُ وَأَصْلِحْ لِي فِي ذُرِّيَّتِي ـ إِنِّي تُبْتُ إِلَيْكَ وَإِنِّي مِنَ الْمُسْلِمِينَ

﴿١٥﴾ أُولَٰئِكَ الَّذِينَ نَتَقَبَّلُ عَنْهُمْ أَحْسَنَ مَا عَمِلُوا وَنَتَجَاوَزُ عَنْ سَيِّئَاتِهِمْ

فِي أَصْحَابِ الْجَنَّةِ ـ وَعْدَ الصِّدْقِ الَّذِي كَانُوا يُوعَدُونَ ﴿١٦﴾ ﴿الأحقاف﴾

We have commanded man to be virtuous unto his parents. His mother carried him in struggle and bore him in struggle, and his bearing and weaning is thirty months, such that when he reaches maturity and reaches forty years he says, "My Lord, inspire me to be thankful for Thy blessing with which Thou hast blessed me and hast blessed my parents, and that I may do what is right such that it pleases Thee; and grant me righteousness in my offspring. Truly I turn in repentance unto Thee, and truly I am among those who surrender" (15) It is they from whom We shall accept the best of what they have done and We shall overlook their evil deeds. (They) shall be among the inhabitants of paradise – the true promise which they were promised (16)

Al-Ahqāf (The Sand Dunes) 46:15-16

وَالَّذِينَ آمَنُوا وَعَمِلُوا الصَّالِحَاتِ وَآمَنُوا بِمَا نُزِّلَ عَلَىٰ مُحَمَّدٍ وَهُوَ الْحَقُّ مِنْ رَبِّهِمْ ۙ كَفَّرَ عَنْهُمْ سَيِّئَاتِهِمْ وَأَصْلَحَ بَالَهُمْ ﴿٢﴾ ﴿محمد﴾

And those who believe and perform righteous deeds, and believe in what has been sent down unto Muhammad – for it is the truth from their Lord – He will absolve them of their evil deeds and will set their hearts at rest (2)

Muhammad (Muhammad) 47:2

يَا أَيُّهَا الَّذِينَ آمَنُوا أَطِيعُوا اللَّهَ وَأَطِيعُوا الرَّسُولَ وَلَا تُبْطِلُوا أَعْمَالَكُمْ ﴿٣٣﴾

﴿محمد﴾

O you who believe! Obey God and obey the Messenger and do not let your (good) deeds be in vain (33)

Muhammad (Muhammad) 47:33

فَلَا تَهِنُوا وَتَدْعُوا إِلَى السَّلْمِ وَأَنْتُمُ الْأَعْلَوْنَ وَاللَّهُ مَعَكُمْ وَلَنْ يَتِرَكُمْ أَعْمَالَكُمْ

﴿٣٥﴾ ﴿محمد﴾

So do not lose heart and call for peace, for you have the upper hand. And God is with you and will not deprive you of your (good) deeds (35)

Muhammad (Muhammad) 47:35

هُوَ الَّذِي أَنْزَلَ السَّكِينَةَ فِي قُلُوبِ الْمُؤْمِنِينَ لِيَزْدَادُوا إِيمَانًا مَعَ إِيمَانِهِمْ ۚ

وَلِلَّهِ جُنُودُ السَّمَاوَاتِ وَالْأَرْضِ ۚ وَكَانَ اللَّهُ عَلِيمًا حَكِيمًا ﴿٤﴾ لِيُدْخِلَ

الْمُؤْمِنِينَ وَالْمُؤْمِنَاتِ جَنَّاتٍ تَجْرِي مِنْ تَحْتِهَا الْأَنْهَارُ خَالِدِينَ فِيهَا وَيُكَفِّرَ

عَنْهُمْ سَيِّئَاتِهِمْ ۚ وَكَانَ ذَلِكَ عِنْدَ اللَّهِ فَوْزًا عَظِيمًا ﴿٥﴾ ﴿الفتح﴾

It is He Who sent down tranquility into the hearts of the believers, so
that they may add faith to their faith. To God belong the forces of the
heavens and the earth, and God is Knowing, Wise (4) That He may admit
the believing men and the believing women into Gardens beneath which
rivers flow abiding therein, and that He may absolve them of their evil
deeds – and that is in the sight of God a great triumph (5)

Al-Fath (Victory) 48:4-5

لَقَدْ رَضِيَ اللَّهُ عَنِ الْمُؤْمِنِينَ إِذْ يُبَايِعُونَكَ تَحْتَ الشَّجَرَةِ فَعَلِمَ مَا فِي
قُلُوبِهِمْ فَأَنْزَلَ السَّكِينَةَ عَلَيْهِمْ وَأَثَابَهُمْ فَتْحًا قَرِيبًا ﴿١٨﴾ ﴿الفتح﴾

Indeed, well-pleased was God with the believers when they pledged their allegiance unto thee (Muhammad) under the tree. He knew what was in their hearts and sent down tranquility upon them and rewarded them with a victory soon to come (18)

Al-Fath (Victory) 48:18

مُحَمَّدٌ رَسُولُ اللَّهِ ۚ وَالَّذِينَ مَعَهُ أَشِدَّاءُ عَلَى الْكُفَّارِ رُحَمَاءُ بَيْنَهُمْ ۖ تَرَاهُمْ رُكَّعًا سُجَّدًا يَبْتَغُونَ فَضْلًا مِنَ اللَّهِ وَرِضْوَانًا ۖ سِيمَاهُمْ فِي وُجُوهِهِم مِنْ أَثَرِ السُّجُودِ ۚ ذَٰلِكَ مَثَلُهُمْ فِي التَّوْرَاةِ ۚ وَمَثَلُهُمْ فِي الْإِنْجِيلِ كَزَرْعٍ أَخْرَجَ شَطْأَهُ فَآزَرَهُ فَاسْتَغْلَظَ فَاسْتَوَىٰ عَلَىٰ سُوقِهِ يُعْجِبُ الزُّرَّاعَ لِيَغِيظَ بِهِمُ الْكُفَّارَ ۗ وَعَدَ اللَّهُ الَّذِينَ آمَنُوا وَعَمِلُوا الصَّالِحَاتِ مِنْهُم مَغْفِرَةً وَأَجْرًا عَظِيمًا ﴿٢٩﴾

﴿الفتح﴾

Muhammad is the Messenger of God and those who are with him are tough against the disbelievers, compassionate to one another. You see them bowing, prostrating, seeking God's favour and acceptance; their marks on their faces are from traces of prostration. This is their parable in the Torah. And their parable in the Gospel is like a seed that sends forth its shoot and strengthens it so that it grows stout and stands firm upon its stem, delighting the sowers, that He may enrage the disbelievers. God has promised those among who believe and perform righteous deeds forgiveness and a great reward (29)

Al-Fath (Victory) 48:29

إِنَّمَا الْمُؤْمِنُونَ إِخْوَةٌ فَأَصْلِحُوا بَيْنَ أَخَوَيْكُمْ ۚ وَاتَّقُوا اللَّهَ لَعَلَّكُمْ تُرْحَمُونَ

﴿١٠﴾ ﴿الحجرات﴾

Truly the believers are brothers, so make peace between your brethren, and be mindful of God, so that you may receive mercy (10)

Al-Hujurāt (The Private Apartments) 49:10

يَا أَيُّهَا النَّاسُ إِنَّا خَلَقْنَاكُمْ مِنْ ذَكَرٍ وَأُنْثَىٰ وَجَعَلْنَاكُمْ شُعُوبًا وَقَبَائِلَ لِتَعَارَفُوا ۚ

إِنَّ أَكْرَمَكُمْ عِنْدَ اللَّهِ أَتْقَاكُمْ ۚ إِنَّ اللَّهَ عَلِيمٌ خَبِيرٌ ﴿١٣﴾ ﴿الحجرات﴾

O mankind! Truly We created you from a male and a female and We made you into nations and tribes so that you may know one another. Truly, the most noble of you in the sight of God is the most mindful. Indeed, God is all All-Knowing and All-Aware (13)

Al-Ḥujurāt (The Private Apartments) 49:13

وَلَقَدْ خَلَقْنَا الْإِنْسَانَ وَنَعْلَمُ مَا تُوَسْوِسُ بِهِ نَفْسُهُ ۖ وَنَحْنُ أَقْرَبُ إِلَيْهِ مِنْ حَبْلِ

الْوَرِيدِ ﴿١٦﴾ ﴿ق﴾

Indeed, We created man and We know what his soul whispers to him; and We are nearer to him than his jugular vein (16)

Qāf (Qaaf) 50:16

وَأُزْلِفَتِ الْجَنَّةُ لِلْمُتَّقِينَ غَيْرَ بَعِيدٍ ﴿٣١﴾ هَٰذَا مَا تُوعَدُونَ لِكُلِّ أَوَّابٍ

حَفِيظٍ ﴿٣٢﴾ مَنْ خَشِيَ الرَّحْمَٰنَ بِالْغَيْبِ وَجَاءَ بِقَلْبٍ مُنِيبٍ ﴿٣٣﴾

ادْخُلُوهَا بِسَلَامٍ ذَٰلِكَ يَوْمُ الْخُلُودِ ﴿٣٤﴾ لَهُم مَّا يَشَاءُونَ فِيهَا وَلَدَيْنَا مَزِيدٌ

﴿ق﴾ ﴿٣٥﴾

And Paradise will be brought near to the God-conscious, no longer distant (31) "This is what you were promised - for everyone who turned to God in sincere remembrance (32) Who stood in awe of the Most Compassionate unseen and comes (before Him) with a contrite heart (33) Enter it in peace. This is the Day of eternal life" (34) They shall have all that they wish for there and with Us there is more (35)

Qāf (Qaaf) 50:31-35

إِنَّ الْمُتَّقِينَ فِي جَنَّاتٍ وَعُيُونٍ ﴿١٥﴾ آخِذِينَ مَا آتَاهُمْ رَبُّهُمْ ۚ إِنَّهُمْ كَانُوا قَبْلَ ذَٰلِكَ مُحْسِنِينَ ﴿١٦﴾ كَانُوا قَلِيلًا مِنَ اللَّيْلِ مَا يَهْجَعُونَ ﴿١٧﴾ وَبِالْأَسْحَارِ هُمْ يَسْتَغْفِرُونَ ﴿١٨﴾ وَفِي أَمْوَالِهِمْ حَقٌّ لِلسَّائِلِ وَالْمَحْرُومِ ﴿١٩﴾ وَفِي الْأَرْضِ آيَاتٌ لِلْمُوقِنِينَ ﴿٢٠﴾ وَفِي أَنْفُسِكُمْ ۚ أَفَلَا تُبْصِرُونَ ﴿٢١﴾ وَفِي السَّمَاءِ رِزْقُكُمْ وَمَا تُوعَدُونَ ﴿٢٢﴾ ﴿الذاريات﴾

Truly the God-conscious shall be amid Gardens and Springs (15) Taking joy in that which their Lord gives them. Truly before then they were virtuous (16) They would sleep but little of the night (17) And in the hour of early dawn would pray for forgiveness (18) And in their wealth is a rightful share for the beggar and the deprived (19) And on the earth are signs for those with inner certainty (20) and within your own selves. Do you then not see? (21) And in Heaven is your provision and all that you were promised (22)

Al-Dhāriyat (Scatterering Winds) 51:15-22

وَٱلسَّمَآءَ بَنَيْنَٰهَا بِأَيْدٍ وَإِنَّا لَمُوسِعُونَ ﴿٤٧﴾ وَٱلْأَرْضَ فَرَشْنَٰهَا فَنِعْمَ ٱلْمَٰهِدُونَ ﴿٤٨﴾ وَمِن كُلِّ شَىْءٍ خَلَقْنَا زَوْجَيْنِ لَعَلَّكُمْ تَذَكَّرُونَ ﴿٤٩﴾ فَفِرُّوا إِلَى ٱللَّهِ إِنِّي لَكُم مِّنْهُ نَذِيرٌ مُّبِينٌ ﴿٥٠﴾ ﴿الذاريات﴾

We have built the Heaven with might, and truly it is We Who make it vast (47) And the earth We have spread out, and how well We have smoothed it (48) And of everything We have created pairs, so that you might be mindful (49) So say, "Hasten to God, I am a clear warner unto you from Him" (50)

Al-Dhāriyat (Scatterering Winds) 51.47-50

إِنَّ الْمُتَّقِينَ فِي جَنَّاتٍ وَنَعِيمٍ ﴿١٧﴾ فَاكِهِينَ بِمَا آتَاهُمْ رَبُّهُمْ وَوَقَاهُمْ رَبُّهُمْ عَذَابَ الْجَحِيمِ ﴿١٨﴾ كُلُوا وَاشْرَبُوا هَنِيئًا بِمَا كُنتُمْ تَعْمَلُونَ ﴿١٩﴾ مُتَّكِئِينَ عَلَىٰ سُرُرٍ مَّصْفُوفَةٍ ۖ وَزَوَّجْنَاهُم بِحُورٍ عِينٍ ﴿٢٠﴾ ﴿الطور﴾

Truly the God-conscious shall be amid Gardens and bliss (17) Rejoicing in what their Lord has given them. And their Lord has shielded them from the torment of the Blaze (18) "Eat and drink in health (as a reward) for what you used to do" (19) Reclining upon couches arrayed, and We shall wed them to beautiful-eyed maidens (20)

Al-Tūr (The Mount) 52:17-20

وَالَّذِينَ آمَنُوا وَاتَّبَعَتْهُمْ ذُرِّيَّتُهُم بِإِيمَانٍ أَلْحَقْنَا بِهِمْ ذُرِّيَّتَهُمْ وَمَا أَلَتْنَاهُم مِّنْ عَمَلِهِم مِّن شَيْءٍ ۚ كُلُّ امْرِئٍ بِمَا كَسَبَ رَهِينٌ ﴿٢١﴾ وَأَمْدَدْنَاهُم بِفَاكِهَةٍ وَلَحْمٍ مِّمَّا يَشْتَهُونَ ﴿٢٢﴾ يَتَنَازَعُونَ فِيهَا كَأْسًا لَّا لَغْوٌ فِيهَا وَلَا تَأْثِيمٌ ﴿٢٣﴾ وَيَطُوفُ عَلَيْهِمْ غِلْمَانٌ لَّهُمْ كَأَنَّهُمْ لُؤْلُؤٌ مَّكْنُونٌ ﴿٢٤﴾ ﴿الطور﴾

And those who believe and whose offspring followed them in faith,
We shall unite them with their offspring and will not deprive them
of nought of their deeds. Every person is a pledge for what he has
earned (21) And We shall bestow upon them fruit and meat such
as they desire (22) They shall pass around a cup wherein is neither idle talk nor sin (23) And there waiting on them are devoted
youths, as if they were hidden pearls (24)

Al-Tūr (The Mount) 52:21-24

وَلِلَّهِ مَا فِي السَّمَاوَاتِ وَمَا فِي الْأَرْضِ لِيَجْزِيَ الَّذِينَ أَسَاءُوا بِمَا عَمِلُوا وَيَجْزِيَ الَّذِينَ أَحْسَنُوا بِالْحُسْنَى ﴿٣١﴾ الَّذِينَ يَجْتَنِبُونَ كَبَائِرَ الْإِثْمِ وَالْفَوَاحِشَ إِلَّا اللَّمَمَ ۚ إِنَّ رَبَّكَ وَاسِعُ الْمَغْفِرَةِ ۚ هُوَ أَعْلَمُ بِكُمْ إِذْ أَنْشَأَكُمْ مِنَ الْأَرْضِ وَإِذْ أَنْتُمْ أَجِنَّةٌ فِي بُطُونِ أُمَّهَاتِكُمْ ۖ فَلَا تُزَكُّوا أَنْفُسَكُمْ ۖ هُوَ أَعْلَمُ بِمَنِ اتَّقَىٰ ﴿٣٢﴾ ﴿النجم﴾

And unto God belongs all that is in the heavens and all that is on the earth, that He will reward those who do evil according to their deeds, and will reward those who do good with goodness (31) Those who avoid grave sins and indecencies, save the slight offences; truly your Lord is of vast forgiveness. He knows you best, from when He created you from the earth and when you were hidden in your mothers' wombs. Therefore ascribe not purity unto yourselves. He knows best who is mindful of Him (32)

Al-Najm (The Star) 53:31-32

لَّا تَزِرُ وَازِرَةٌ وِزْرَ أُخْرَىٰ ﴿٣٨﴾ وَأَن لَّيْسَ لِلْإِنسَانِ إِلَّا مَا سَعَىٰ ﴿٣٩﴾ وَأَنَّ سَعْيَهُ سَوْفَ يُرَىٰ ﴿٤٠﴾ ثُمَّ يُجْزَاهُ الْجَزَاءَ الْأَوْفَىٰ ﴿٤١﴾ وَأَنَّ إِلَىٰ رَبِّكَ الْمُنتَهَىٰ ﴿٤٢﴾ وَأَنَّهُ هُوَ أَضْحَكَ وَأَبْكَىٰ ﴿٤٣﴾ وَأَنَّهُ هُوَ أَمَاتَ وَأَحْيَا ﴿٤٤﴾ وَأَنَّهُ خَلَقَ الزَّوْجَيْنِ الذَّكَرَ وَالْأُنثَىٰ ﴿٤٥﴾ مِن نُّطْفَةٍ إِذَا تُمْنَىٰ ﴿٤٦﴾ وَأَنَّ عَلَيْهِ النَّشْأَةَ الْأُخْرَىٰ ﴿٤٧﴾ وَأَنَّهُ هُوَ أَغْنَىٰ وَأَقْنَىٰ ﴿٤٨﴾ وَأَنَّهُ هُوَ رَبُّ الشِّعْرَىٰ ﴿٤٩﴾ ﴿النجم﴾

None shall bear the burden of another (38) And that man shall have nought but what he has stived (39) And that his striving shall be seen (40) Whereupon he shall be rewarded for it with the fullest reward (41) And that (the return to) thy Lord is the final goal (42) And that it is He Who makes you laugh and weep (43) And that it is He Who causes death and life (44) And that He created in pairs - the male and the female (45) From a drop (of sperm) when it is poured forth (46) And that with Him lies another coming of life (47) And that it is He Who gives wealth and contentment (48) And that it is He Who is the Lord of Sirius (49)

Al-Najm (The Star) 53:38-49

339

إِنَّ الْمُتَّقِينَ فِي جَنَّاتٍ وَنَهَرٍ ﴿٥٤﴾ فِي مَقْعَدِ صِدْقٍ عِنْدَ مَلِيكٍ مُقْتَدِرٍ
﴿٥٥﴾ ﴿القمر﴾

Truly the God-conscious will be amid Gardens and rivers (54) Established on a seat of truth before an Omnipotent Sovereign (55)

Al-Qamar (The Moon) 54:54-55

الرَّحْمَنُ ﴿١﴾ عَلَّمَ الْقُرْآنَ ﴿٢﴾ خَلَقَ الْإِنْسَانَ ﴿٣﴾ عَلَّمَهُ الْبَيَانَ ﴿٤﴾ الشَّمْسُ وَالْقَمَرُ بِحُسْبَانٍ ﴿٥﴾ وَالنَّجْمُ وَالشَّجَرُ يَسْجُدَانِ ﴿٦﴾ وَالسَّمَاءَ رَفَعَهَا وَوَضَعَ الْمِيزَانَ ﴿٧﴾ أَلَّا تَطْغَوْا فِي الْمِيزَانِ ﴿٨﴾ وَأَقِيمُوا الْوَزْنَ بِالْقِسْطِ وَلَا تُخْسِرُوا الْمِيزَانَ ﴿٩﴾ وَالْأَرْضَ وَضَعَهَا لِلْأَنَامِ ﴿١٠﴾ فِيهَا فَاكِهَةٌ وَالنَّخْلُ ذَاتُ الْأَكْمَامِ ﴿١١﴾ وَالْحَبُّ ذُو الْعَصْفِ وَالرَّيْحَانُ ﴿١٢﴾ ﴿الرحمن﴾

The Compassionate (1) He taught the Qur'an (2) He created man (3) Has taught him speech (4) The sun and the moon run their appointed courses (5) And the stars and the trees prostrate (6) And the sky He has raised and He has set the balance (7) That you do not exceed in the balance (8) So set the weight with justice and do not fall short in the balance (9) And the earth He laid down for (His) creatures (10) Therein are fruit and date palms with sheathed clusters (11) And husked grain and fragrant herbs (12)

Al-Rahmān (The Compassionate) 55:1-12

وَلِمَنْ خَافَ مَقَامَ رَبِّهِ جَنَّتَانِ ﴿٤٦﴾ فَبِأَيِّ آلَاءِ رَبِّكُمَا تُكَذِّبَانِ ﴿٤٧﴾ ذَوَاتَا أَفْنَانٍ ﴿٤٨﴾ فَبِأَيِّ آلَاءِ رَبِّكُمَا تُكَذِّبَانِ ﴿٤٩﴾ فِيهِمَا عَيْنَانِ تَجْرِيَانِ ﴿٥٠﴾ فَبِأَيِّ آلَاءِ رَبِّكُمَا تُكَذِّبَانِ ﴿٥١﴾ فِيهِمَا مِنْ كُلِّ فَاكِهَةٍ زَوْجَانِ ﴿٥٢﴾ فَبِأَيِّ آلَاءِ رَبِّكُمَا تُكَذِّبَانِ ﴿٥٣﴾ مُتَّكِئِينَ عَلَىٰ فُرُشٍ بَطَائِنُهَا مِنْ إِسْتَبْرَقٍ ۚ وَجَنَى الْجَنَّتَيْنِ دَانٍ ﴿٥٤﴾ فَبِأَيِّ آلَاءِ رَبِّكُمَا تُكَذِّبَانِ ﴿٥٥﴾ فِيهِنَّ قَاصِرَاتُ الطَّرْفِ لَمْ يَطْمِثْهُنَّ إِنْسٌ قَبْلَهُمْ وَلَا جَانٌّ ﴿٥٦﴾ فَبِأَيِّ آلَاءِ رَبِّكُمَا تُكَذِّبَانِ ﴿٥٧﴾ كَأَنَّهُنَّ الْيَاقُوتُ وَالْمَرْجَانُ ﴿٥٨﴾ فَبِأَيِّ آلَاءِ رَبِّكُمَا تُكَذِّبَانِ ﴿٥٩﴾ هَلْ جَزَاءُ الْإِحْسَانِ إِلَّا الْإِحْسَانُ ﴿٦٠﴾ فَبِأَيِّ آلَاءِ رَبِّكُمَا تُكَذِّبَانِ ﴿٦١﴾ وَمِنْ دُونِهِمَا جَنَّتَانِ ﴿٦٢﴾ فَبِأَيِّ آلَاءِ رَبِّكُمَا تُكَذِّبَانِ ﴿٦٣﴾ مُدْهَامَّتَانِ ﴿٦٤﴾ فَبِأَيِّ آلَاءِ رَبِّكُمَا تُكَذِّبَانِ ﴿٦٥﴾ فِيهِمَا عَيْنَانِ نَضَّاخَتَانِ ﴿٦٦﴾ فَبِأَيِّ آلَاءِ رَبِّكُمَا تُكَذِّبَانِ ﴿٦٧﴾ فِيهِمَا فَاكِهَةٌ وَنَخْلٌ وَرُمَّانٌ ﴿٦٨﴾ فَبِأَيِّ آلَاءِ رَبِّكُمَا تُكَذِّبَانِ ﴿٦٩﴾ فِيهِنَّ خَيْرَاتٌ حِسَانٌ ﴿٧٠﴾ فَبِأَيِّ آلَاءِ رَبِّكُمَا تُكَذِّبَانِ ﴿٧١﴾ حُورٌ مَقْصُورَاتٌ فِي الْخِيَامِ ﴿٧٢﴾ فَبِأَيِّ آلَاءِ رَبِّكُمَا تُكَذِّبَانِ ﴿٧٣﴾ لَمْ يَطْمِثْهُنَّ إِنْسٌ قَبْلَهُمْ وَلَا جَانٌّ ﴿٧٤﴾ فَبِأَيِّ آلَاءِ رَبِّكُمَا تُكَذِّبَانِ ﴿٧٥﴾ مُتَّكِئِينَ عَلَىٰ رَفْرَفٍ خُضْرٍ وَعَبْقَرِيٍّ حِسَانٍ ﴿٧٦﴾ فَبِأَيِّ آلَاءِ رَبِّكُمَا تُكَذِّبَانِ ﴿٧٧﴾ تَبَارَكَ اسْمُ رَبِّكَ ذِي الْجَلَالِ وَالْإِكْرَامِ ﴿٧٨﴾ ﴿الرحمن﴾

And for the one who fears standing before his Lord, there are two Gardens (46) Which then of your Lord's favours do you deny? (47) With green branches (48) Which then of your Lord's favours do you deny? (49) In each are two flowing springs (50) Which then of your Lord's favours do you deny? (51) In each are two kinds of every fruit (52) Which then of your Lord's favours do you deny? (53) Reclining upon beds lined with rich brocade, the fruit of both Gardens near to hand (54) Which then of your Lord's favours do you deny? (55) Therein are maidens of modest gaze, untouched before by man nor jinn (56) Which then of your Lord's favours do you deny? (57) They are like rubies and coral (58) Which then of your Lord's favours do you deny? (59) Could there be any other reward for goodness other than goodness? (60) Which then of your Lord's favours do you deny? (61) And besides these two there are two (other) Gardens (62) Which then of your Lord's favours do you deny? (63) Of the deepest green (64) Which then of your Lord's favours do you deny? (65) In each are two gushing springs (66) Which then of your Lord's favours do you deny? (67) In both are fruit, date palm and pomegranate (68) Which then of your Lord's favours do you deny? (69) Therein is good and beauty (70) Which then of your Lord's favours do you deny? (71) Maidens sheltered in pavilions (72) Which then of your Lord's favours do you deny? (73) Untouched before by man nor jinn (74) Which then of your Lord's favours do you deny? (75) Reclining upon green cushions and fine carpets (76) Which then of your Lord's favours do you deny? (77) Blessed is the Name of Thy Lord, full of Majesty and Honour (78)

Al-Rahmān (The Compassionate) 55:46-78

إِنَّهُ لَقُرْآنٌ كَرِيمٌ ﴿٧٧﴾ فِي كِتَابٍ مَكْنُونٍ ﴿٧٨﴾ لَا يَمَسُّهُ إِلَّا الْمُطَهَّرُونَ ﴿٧٩﴾ تَنْزِيلٌ مِنْ رَبِّ الْعَالَمِينَ ﴿٨٠﴾ ﴿الواقعة﴾

Truly it is a Noble Qur'an (77) In a Book well-guarded (78) Which none can touch save the purified (79) A revelation from the Lord of the Worlds (80)

Al-Wāqi'ah (The Imminent) 56:77-80

آمِنُوا بِاللَّهِ وَرَسُولِهِ وَأَنْفِقُوا مِمَّا جَعَلَكُم مُّسْتَخْلَفِينَ فِيهِ فَالَّذِينَ آمَنُوا مِنْكُمْ وَأَنْفَقُوا لَهُمْ أَجْرٌ كَبِيرٌ ﴿٧﴾ ﴿الحديد﴾

Believe in God and His Messenger and spend (in charity) of that which He has made you trustees. Those of you who believe and spend (in charity), theirs will be a great reward (7)

Al-Ḥadīd (Iron) 57:7

هُوَ الَّذِي يُنَزِّلُ عَلَىٰ عَبْدِهِ آيَاتٍ بَيِّنَاتٍ لِيُخْرِجَكُمْ مِنَ الظُّلُمَاتِ إِلَى النُّورِ
وَإِنَّ اللَّهَ بِكُمْ لَرَءُوفٌ رَحِيمٌ ﴿٩﴾ ﴿الحديد﴾

It is He Who sends down clear signs upon His servant to bring you out
of the depths of darkness into the light, and truly God is most Compassionate and Merciful to you (9)

Al-Ḥadīd (Iron) 57:9

مَن ذَا الَّذِي يُقْرِضُ اللَّهَ قَرْضًا حَسَنًا فَيُضَاعِفَهُ لَهُ وَلَهُ أَجْرٌ كَرِيمٌ ﴿١١﴾

﴿الحديد﴾

Who is it that will loan God a beautiful loan? Indeed (God) will increase
it for him and he will have a generous reward (11)

Al-Hadīd (Iron) 57:11

يَوْمَ تَرَى الْمُؤْمِنِينَ وَالْمُؤْمِنَاتِ يَسْعَىٰ نُورُهُم بَيْنَ أَيْدِيهِمْ وَبِأَيْمَانِهِم بُشْرَاكُمُ

الْيَوْمَ جَنَّاتٌ تَجْرِي مِن تَحْتِهَا الْأَنْهَارُ خَالِدِينَ فِيهَا ۚ ذَٰلِكَ هُوَ الْفَوْزُ الْعَظِيمُ

﴿١٢﴾ ﴿الحديد﴾

On the Day when you (Muhammad) will see the believing men and the believing women with their light spreading before them and on their right, "Glad tidings upon you on this Day; Gardens beneath which rivers flow abiding therein. That is the supreme triumph" (12)

Al-Hadīd (Iron) 57:12

سَابِقُوا إِلَىٰ مَغْفِرَةٍ مِنْ رَبِّكُمْ وَجَنَّةٍ عَرْضُهَا كَعَرْضِ السَّمَاءِ وَالْأَرْضِ أُعِدَّتْ لِلَّذِينَ آمَنُوا بِاللَّهِ وَرُسُلِهِ ۚ ذَٰلِكَ فَضْلُ اللَّهِ يُؤْتِيهِ مَنْ يَشَاءُ ۚ وَاللَّهُ ذُو الْفَضْلِ الْعَظِيمِ ﴿٢١﴾ ﴿الحديد﴾

Race unto forgiveness from your Lord and to a Garden the breadth of which is as the breadth of Heaven and earth, prepared for those who believe in God and His messengers. That is God's bounty, which He gives to whomever He will, and God is of Infinite Bounty (21)

Al-Hadīd (Iron) 57:21

ما أَصابَ مِن مُصيبَةٍ فِي الأَرضِ وَلا فِي أَنفُسِكُم إِلّا فِي كِتابٍ مِن قَبلِ

أَن نَبرَأَها ۚ إِنَّ ذٰلِكَ عَلَى اللَّهِ يَسيرٌ ﴿٢٢﴾ ﴿الحديد﴾

No misfortune befalls the earth or yourselves, but is recorded in a decree
before We bring it into existence. Truly that is easy for God (22)

Al-Hadīd (Iron) 57:22

يَا أَيُّهَا الَّذِينَ آمَنُوا اتَّقُوا اللَّهَ وَآمِنُوا بِرَسُولِهِ يُؤْتِكُمْ كِفْلَيْنِ مِنْ رَحْمَتِهِ وَيَجْعَلْ لَكُمْ نُورًا تَمْشُونَ بِهِ وَيَغْفِرْ لَكُمْ ۚ وَاللَّهُ غَفُورٌ رَحِيمٌ ﴿٢٨﴾ ﴿الحديد﴾

O you who believe! Be mindful of God and believe in His Messenger, He will give you a double portion of His Mercy and will provide for you a light to walk upon, and will forgive you. For God is Forgiving, Merciful (28)

Al-Hadīd (Iron) 57:28

لِئَلَّا يَعْلَمَ أَهْلُ الْكِتَابِ أَلَّا يَقْدِرُونَ عَلَىٰ شَيْءٍ مِنْ فَضْلِ اللَّهِ ، وَأَنَّ الْفَضْلَ بِيَدِ اللَّهِ يُؤْتِيهِ مَنْ يَشَاءُ ۚ وَاللَّهُ ذُو الْفَضْلِ الْعَظِيمِ ﴿٢٩﴾ ﴿الحديد﴾

That the People of the Scripture may know that they have no power over any of God's Bounty, and that the Bounty is in God's Hand (alone) to give to whom He will, and God is of Infinite Bounty (29)

Al-Hadīd (Iron) 57:29

يَا أَيُّهَا الَّذِينَ آمَنُوا إِذَا تَنَاجَيْتُمْ فَلَا تَتَنَاجَوْا بِالْإِثْمِ وَالْعُدْوَانِ وَمَعْصِيَتِ الرَّسُولِ وَتَنَاجَوْا بِالْبِرِّ وَالتَّقْوَىٰ ـ وَاتَّقُوا اللَّهَ الَّذِي إِلَيْهِ تُحْشَرُونَ ﴿٩﴾ إِنَّمَا النَّجْوَىٰ مِنَ الشَّيْطَانِ لِيَحْزُنَ الَّذِينَ آمَنُوا وَلَيْسَ بِضَارِّهِمْ شَيْئًا إِلَّا بِإِذْنِ اللَّهِ ۚ وَعَلَى اللَّهِ فَلْيَتَوَكَّلِ الْمُؤْمِنُونَ ﴿١٠﴾ ﴿المجادلة﴾

O you who believe! When you converse in secret, do not converse in secret to be sinful, hostile and disobedient to the Messenger; converse in secret in a way that is pious and mindful. And be mindful of God unto Whom you shall be gathered (9) Truly conspiracy is only from Satan, so that those who believe may grieve, yet he cannot harm them in the least, save by God's Leave. And in God let the believers put their trust (10)

Al-Mujādilah (The Pleading) 58:9-10

لَا تَجِدُ قَوْمًا يُؤْمِنُونَ بِاللَّهِ وَالْيَوْمِ الْآخِرِ يُوَادُّونَ مَنْ حَادَّ اللَّهَ وَرَسُولَهُ وَلَوْ
كَانُوا آبَاءَهُمْ أَوْ أَبْنَاءَهُمْ أَوْ إِخْوَانَهُمْ أَوْ عَشِيرَتَهُمْ ۚ أُولَئِكَ كَتَبَ فِي قُلُوبِهِمُ
الْإِيمَانَ وَأَيَّدَهُمْ بِرُوحٍ مِنْهُ ۖ وَيُدْخِلُهُمْ جَنَّاتٍ تَجْرِي مِنْ تَحْتِهَا الْأَنْهَارُ
خَالِدِينَ فِيهَا ۚ رَضِيَ اللَّهُ عَنْهُمْ وَرَضُوا عَنْهُ ۚ أُولَئِكَ حِزْبُ اللَّهِ ۚ أَلَا إِنَّ حِزْبَ
اللَّهِ هُمُ الْمُفْلِحُونَ ﴿٢٢﴾ ﴿المجادلة﴾

You shall not find people who (truly) believe in God and the Last Day loving those who oppose God and His Messenger, even if they be their fathers or their sons or their brothers or their clan. It is they in whose hearts God has inscribed faith and strengthened them with a Spirit from Him. He will admit them into Gardens beneath which rivers flow, abiding therein. God is content with them and they content with Him. They are the people of God. Lo! Truly the people of God are the ones who shall prosper (22)

Al-Mujādilah (The Pleading) 58:22

يَوْمَ يَجْمَعُكُمْ لِيَوْمِ الْجَمْعِ ـ ذَلِكَ يَوْمُ التَّغَابُنِ ـ وَمَنْ يُؤْمِنْ بِاللَّهِ وَيَعْمَلْ

صَالِحًا يُكَفِّرْ عَنْهُ سَيِّئَاتِهِ وَيُدْخِلْهُ جَنَّاتٍ تَجْرِي مِنْ تَحْتِهَا الْأَنْهَارُ خَالِدِينَ

فِيهَا أَبَدًا ـ ذَلِكَ الْفَوْزُ الْعَظِيمُ ﴿٩﴾ ﴿التغابن﴾

The day that He shall gather you unto the Day of Gathering, that will be the Day of Dispossession. And whoever believes in God and performs righteous deeds, will be absolved of all evil deeds and He will bring them into Gardens beneath which rivers flow abiding therein forever. That is the supreme triumph (9)

Al-Taghābun (Dispossession) 64:9

مَا أَصَابَ مِنْ مُصِيبَةٍ إِلَّا بِإِذْنِ اللَّهِ ۗ وَمَنْ يُؤْمِنْ بِاللَّهِ يَهْدِ قَلْبَهُ ۚ وَاللَّهُ بِكُلِّ

شَيْءٍ عَلِيمٌ ﴿١١﴾ ﴿التغابن﴾

No calamity can befall (anyone), save by God's Leave. And whoever believes in God, He guides his heart. And God is Knower of all things (11)

Al-Taghābun (Dispossession) 64:11

اللَّهُ لَا إِلَهَ إِلَّا هُوَ ۚ وَعَلَى اللَّهِ فَلْيَتَوَكَّلِ الْمُؤْمِنُونَ ﴿١٣﴾ ﴿التغابن﴾

God, there is no god but Him, and in God let the believers put their trust (13)

Al-Taghābun (Dispossession) 64:13

إِنْ تُقْرِضُوا اللَّهَ قَرْضًا حَسَنًا يُضَاعِفْهُ لَكُمْ وَيَغْفِرْ لَكُمْ ۚ وَاللَّهُ شَكُورٌ حَلِيمٌ

﴿١٦﴾ ﴿التغابن﴾

And if you lend unto God a goodly loan, He will multiply it for you and forgive you. And God is Thankful, Forbearing (16)

Al-Taghābun (Dispossession) 64:16

يَا أَيُّهَا الَّذِينَ آمَنُوا تُوبُوا إِلَى اللَّهِ تَوْبَةً نَصُوحًا عَسَىٰ رَبُّكُمْ أَنْ يُكَفِّرَ عَنْكُمْ سَيِّئَاتِكُمْ وَيُدْخِلَكُمْ جَنَّاتٍ تَجْرِي مِنْ تَحْتِهَا الْأَنْهَارُ يَوْمَ لَا يُخْزِي اللَّهُ النَّبِيَّ وَالَّذِينَ آمَنُوا مَعَهُ ـ نُورُهُمْ يَسْعَىٰ بَيْنَ أَيْدِيهِمْ وَبِأَيْمَانِهِمْ يَقُولُونَ رَبَّنَا أَتْمِمْ لَنَا نُورَنَا وَاغْفِرْ لَنَا ـ إِنَّكَ عَلَىٰ كُلِّ شَيْءٍ قَدِيرٌ ﴿٨﴾ ﴿التحريم﴾

O you who believe! Repent unto God with sincere repentance. It may be that your Lord will absolve you of your evil deeds and will admit you into Gardens beneath which rivers flow on a Day when God will not disgrace the Prophet and those who believed with him. Their light will spread out before them and to their right, they will say "Our Lord! Perfect our light for us and forgive us. Truly You are Powerful over all things" (8)

Al Tahrīm (The Prohibition) 66:8

إِنَّ الْإِنْسَانَ خُلِقَ هَلُوعًا ﴿١٩﴾ إِذَا مَسَّهُ الشَّرُّ جَزُوعًا ﴿٢٠﴾ وَإِذَا مَسَّهُ الْخَيْرُ مَنُوعًا ﴿٢١﴾ إِلَّا الْمُصَلِّينَ ﴿٢٢﴾ الَّذِينَ هُمْ عَلَىٰ صَلَاتِهِمْ دَائِمُونَ ﴿٢٣﴾ وَالَّذِينَ فِي أَمْوَالِهِمْ حَقٌّ مَعْلُومٌ ﴿٢٤﴾ لِلسَّائِلِ وَالْمَحْرُومِ ﴿٢٥﴾ وَالَّذِينَ يُصَدِّقُونَ بِيَوْمِ الدِّينِ ﴿٢٦﴾ وَالَّذِينَ هُمْ مِنْ عَذَابِ رَبِّهِمْ مُشْفِقُونَ ﴿٢٧﴾ إِنَّ عَذَابَ رَبِّهِمْ غَيْرُ مَأْمُونٍ ﴿٢٨﴾ وَالَّذِينَ هُمْ لِفُرُوجِهِمْ حَافِظُونَ ﴿٢٩﴾ إِلَّا عَلَىٰ أَزْوَاجِهِمْ أَوْ مَا مَلَكَتْ أَيْمَانُهُمْ فَإِنَّهُمْ غَيْرُ مَلُومِينَ ﴿٣٠﴾ فَمَنِ ابْتَغَىٰ وَرَاءَ ذَٰلِكَ فَأُولَٰئِكَ هُمُ الْعَادُونَ ﴿٣١﴾ وَالَّذِينَ هُمْ لِأَمَانَاتِهِمْ وَعَهْدِهِمْ رَاعُونَ ﴿٣٢﴾ وَالَّذِينَ هُمْ بِشَهَادَاتِهِمْ قَائِمُونَ ﴿٣٣﴾ وَالَّذِينَ هُمْ عَلَىٰ صَلَاتِهِمْ يُحَافِظُونَ ﴿٣٤﴾ أُولَٰئِكَ فِي جَنَّاتٍ مُكْرَمُونَ ﴿٣٥﴾ ﴿المعارج﴾

Truly man was created anxious (19) When misfortune befalls him, fretful (20) And when good fortune befalls him, selfish (21) Save those who pray (22) And are constant in their prayers (23) And those in whose wealth is a recognized right (24) To the beggar and the deprived (25) Who believe in the Day of Judgement (26) And those who fear the punishment of their Lord (27) Truly from the punishment of their Lord non can feel secure (28) And who guard their modesty (29) Save from their spouses or those whom their right hand possess, for this they are not to blame (30) But those who seek beyond that, they are truly transgressors (31) Those who are faithful to their trusts and their oath (32) And those who stand by their testimony (33) And those who are steadfast in their prayer (34) Those shall be honoured in Gardens (of paradise) (35)

Al-Maārij (The Ways of Ascent) 70:19-35

إِنَّ رَبَّكَ يَعْلَمُ أَنَّكَ تَقُومُ أَدْنَىٰ مِنْ ثُلُثَيِ اللَّيْلِ وَنِصْفَهُ وَثُلُثَهُ وَطَائِفَةٌ مِنَ

الَّذِينَ مَعَكَ ۚ وَاللَّهُ يُقَدِّرُ اللَّيْلَ وَالنَّهَارَ ۚ عَلِمَ أَنْ لَنْ تُحْصُوهُ فَتَابَ عَلَيْكُمْ ۖ

فَاقْرَءُوا مَا تَيَسَّرَ مِنَ الْقُرْآنِ ۚ عَلِمَ أَنْ سَيَكُونُ مِنْكُمْ مَرْضَىٰ ۙ وَآخَرُونَ

يَضْرِبُونَ فِي الْأَرْضِ يَبْتَغُونَ مِنْ فَضْلِ اللَّهِ ۙ وَآخَرُونَ يُقَاتِلُونَ فِي سَبِيلِ

اللَّهِ ۖ فَاقْرَءُوا مَا تَيَسَّرَ مِنْهُ ۚ وَأَقِيمُوا الصَّلَاةَ وَآتُوا الزَّكَاةَ وَأَقْرِضُوا اللَّهَ قَرْضًا

حَسَنًا ۚ وَمَا تُقَدِّمُوا لِأَنْفُسِكُمْ مِنْ خَيْرٍ تَجِدُوهُ عِنْدَ اللَّهِ هُوَ خَيْرًا وَأَعْظَمَ

أَجْرًا ۚ وَاسْتَغْفِرُوا اللَّهَ ۖ إِنَّ اللَّهَ غَفُورٌ رَحِيمٌ ﴿٢٠﴾ ﴿المزمل﴾

Truly your Lord knows that you stand vigil well into two-thirds of the night, or half of it, or a third of it, as do a group of those who follow you: and God measures the night and the day. He knows that you will not be able to keep count of it and so He turned to you in mercy. Recite then (as much as you can of) what is easy for you of the Qur'an. He knows that some among you will be sick, and others travelling through the land seeking God's Grace, and others will be fighting in God's cause. So recite as much as what is easy of it (the Qur'an) and be steadfast in prayer and give the alms, and lend unto God a goodly loan - and whatever good you send forth for yourselves, you will find it with God, He is better and greater in reward. And seek God's Forgiveness. Truly God is Forgiving, Merciful (20)

Al-Muzzammil (The Enwarpped) 73:20

يَا أَيُّهَا الْمُدَّثِّرُ ﴿١﴾ قُمْ فَأَنْذِرْ ﴿٢﴾ وَرَبَّكَ فَكَبِّرْ ﴿٣﴾ وَثِيَابَكَ فَطَهِّرْ ﴿٤﴾ وَالرُّجْزَ فَاهْجُرْ ﴿٥﴾ وَلَا تَمْنُنْ تَسْتَكْثِرُ ﴿٦﴾ وَلِرَبِّكَ فَاصْبِرْ ﴿٧﴾

﴿المدثر﴾

O thou enfolded (in thy cloak) (1) Arise and warn! (2) And thy Lord magnify! (3) And thyself purify! (4) And all abomination shun! (5) And show not favour in seeking (worldly) gain! (6) And for the sake of thy Lord be patient (7)

Al-Muddaththir (The Enfolded) 74:1-7

إِنَّ الْأَبْرَارَ يَشْرَبُونَ مِنْ كَأْسٍ كَانَ مِزَاجُهَا كَافُورًا ﴿٥﴾ عَيْنًا يَشْرَبُ بِهَا عِبَادُ اللَّهِ يُفَجِّرُونَهَا تَفْجِيرًا ﴿٦﴾ يُوفُونَ بِالنَّذْرِ وَيَخَافُونَ يَوْمًا كَانَ شَرُّهُ مُسْتَطِيرًا ﴿٧﴾ وَيُطْعِمُونَ الطَّعَامَ عَلَىٰ حُبِّهِ مِسْكِينًا وَيَتِيمًا وَأَسِيرًا ﴿٨﴾ إِنَّمَا نُطْعِمُكُمْ لِوَجْهِ اللَّهِ لَا نُرِيدُ مِنْكُمْ جَزَاءً وَلَا شُكُورًا ﴿٩﴾ إِنَّا نَخَافُ مِنْ رَبِّنَا يَوْمًا عَبُوسًا قَمْطَرِيرًا ﴿١٠﴾ فَوَقَاهُمُ اللَّهُ شَرَّ ذَٰلِكَ الْيَوْمِ وَلَقَّاهُمْ نَضْرَةً وَسُرُورًا ﴿١١﴾ وَجَزَاهُمْ بِمَا صَبَرُوا جَنَّةً وَحَرِيرًا ﴿١٢﴾ مُتَّكِئِينَ فِيهَا عَلَى الْأَرَائِكِ لَا يَرَوْنَ فِيهَا شَمْسًا وَلَا زَمْهَرِيرًا ﴿١٣﴾ وَدَانِيَةً عَلَيْهِمْ ظِلَالُهَا وَذُلِّلَتْ قُطُوفُهَا تَذْلِيلًا ﴿١٤﴾ وَيُطَافُ عَلَيْهِمْ بِآنِيَةٍ مِنْ فِضَّةٍ وَأَكْوَابٍ كَانَتْ قَوَارِيرَا ﴿١٥﴾ قَوَارِيرَ مِنْ فِضَّةٍ قَدَّرُوهَا تَقْدِيرًا ﴿١٦﴾ وَيُسْقَوْنَ فِيهَا كَأْسًا كَانَ مِزَاجُهَا زَنْجَبِيلًا ﴿١٧﴾ عَيْنًا فِيهَا تُسَمَّىٰ سَلْسَبِيلًا ﴿١٨﴾ وَيَطُوفُ عَلَيْهِمْ وِلْدَانٌ مُخَلَّدُونَ إِذَا رَأَيْتَهُمْ حَسِبْتَهُمْ لُؤْلُؤًا مَنْثُورًا ﴿١٩﴾ وَإِذَا رَأَيْتَ ثَمَّ رَأَيْتَ نَعِيمًا وَمُلْكًا كَبِيرًا ﴿٢٠﴾ عَالِيَهُمْ ثِيَابُ سُنْدُسٍ خُضْرٌ وَإِسْتَبْرَقٌ وَحُلُّوا أَسَاوِرَ مِنْ فِضَّةٍ وَسَقَاهُمْ رَبُّهُمْ شَرَابًا طَهُورًا ﴿٢١﴾ إِنَّ هَٰذَا كَانَ لَكُمْ جَزَاءً وَكَانَ سَعْيُكُمْ مَشْكُورًا ﴿٢٢﴾ ﴿الإنسان﴾

Truly the pious shall drink from a cup flavoured with camphor (5) A spring wherefrom the servants of God drink, making it flow through abundantly (6) They fulfill their vows and fear a day when evil is spread far and wide (7) And give food, despite loving it (themselves), to the needy, the orphan and the captive (8) "We feed you only for the sake of God. We do not desire from you reward nor thanks (9) Truly we fear from our Lord a bleak, fateful Day" (10) So God shielded them from the evil of that Day and gave them brightness and joy (11) And rewarded them for their pateince with a Garden and silk (garments) (12) Reclining upon couches feeling thercin neither (scorching) sun nor bitter cold (13) And the shade will come close above them, and clusters of fruit hang low (14) And they will be waited upon with vessels of silver and goblets of crystal (15) Goblets of silver that they have measured (16) Therein they are given a drink flavoured with ginger (17) A spring therein named Salsabil (18) Immortal youths wait upon them; when thou seest them thou wouldst think them scattered pearls (19) And when thou seest, thou wilt see bliss and a great realm (20) Upon them are garments of fine green silk and rich brocade. They will be adorned with bracelets of silver and their Lord shall give them to drink a drink most pure (21) Truly this is a reward for you, and your endeavour is appreciated (22)

Al-Insān (Man) 76:5-22

إِنَّا نَحْنُ نَزَّلْنَا عَلَيْكَ الْقُرْآنَ تَنْزِيلًا ﴿٢٣﴾ فَاصْبِرْ لِحُكْمِ رَبِّكَ وَلَا تُطِعْ
مِنْهُمْ آثِمًا أَوْ كَفُورًا ﴿٢٤﴾ ﴿الإنسان﴾

Truly We have sent down the Qur'an in stages (23) So wait patiently for the judgement of your Lord and obey not among them any sinner or disbeliever (24)

Al-Insān (Man) 76:23-24

وَاذْكُرِ اسْمَ رَبِّكَ بُكْرَةً وَأَصِيلًا ﴿٢٥﴾ وَمِنَ اللَّيْلِ فَاسْجُدْ لَهُ وَسَبِّحْهُ لَيْلًا طَوِيلاً ﴿٢٦﴾ ﴿الإنسان﴾

And remember thy Lord's name, morning and evening (25) And part of the night prostrate to Him and glorify Him by night at length (26)

Al-Insān (Man) 76:25-26

إِنَّ الْمُتَّقِينَ فِي ظِلَالٍ وَعُيُونٍ ﴿٤١﴾ وَفَوَاكِهَ مِمَّا يَشْتَهُونَ ﴿٤٢﴾ كُلُوا

وَاشْرَبُوا هَنِيئًا بِمَا كُنتُمْ تَعْمَلُونَ ﴿٤٣﴾ إِنَّا كَذَٰلِكَ نَجْزِي الْمُحْسِنِينَ

﴿٤٤﴾ ﴿المرسلات﴾

Truly the God-conscious shall be amid shades and springs (41) And (shall have) fruits as they may desire (42) "Eat and drink in enjoyment for what you used to do" (43) Thus do We reward the virtuous (44)

Al-Mursalāt (Those Sent Forth) 77:41-44

إِنَّ لِلْمُتَّقِينَ مَفَازًا ﴿٣١﴾ حَدَائِقَ وَأَعْنَابًا ﴿٣٢﴾ وَكَوَاعِبَ أَتْرَابًا ﴿٣٣﴾ وَكَأْسًا دِهَاقًا ﴿٣٤﴾ لَا يَسْمَعُونَ فِيهَا لَغْوًا وَلَا كِذَّابًا ﴿٣٥﴾ جَزَاءً مِنْ رَبِّكَ عَطَاءً حِسَابًا ﴿٣٦﴾ رَبِّ السَّمَاوَاتِ وَالْأَرْضِ وَمَا بَيْنَهُمَا الرَّحْمَٰنِ ـ لَا يَمْلِكُونَ مِنْهُ خِطَابًا ﴿٣٧﴾ يَوْمَ يَقُومُ الرُّوحُ وَالْمَلَائِكَةُ صَفًّا ـ لَا يَتَكَلَّمُونَ إِلَّا مَنْ أَذِنَ لَهُ الرَّحْمَٰنُ وَقَالَ صَوَابًا ﴿٣٨﴾ ذَٰلِكَ الْيَوْمُ الْحَقُّ ـ فَمَنْ شَاءَ اتَّخَذَ إِلَىٰ رَبِّهِ مَآبًا ﴿٣٩﴾ ﴿النبأ﴾

Truly for the God-conscious is a supreme fulfilment (31) Gardens and vineyards (32) Companions of similar age (33) And an overflowing cup (34) They hear therein no frivolity nor lying (35) A reward from your Lord, a gift abounding (36) Lord of the heavens and the earth and whatever is between them, the Compassionate, none shall have power to address Him (37) On the Day when the Spirit and the angels stand in rows, none shall speak, save those whom the Compassionate permits and who (only) speaks what is right (38) That is the Day of Truth. So whoso will should seek a path of return unto his Lord (39)

Al-Naba (The Tiding) 78:31-39

وَأَمَّا مَنْ خَافَ مَقَامَ رَبِّهِ وَنَهَى النَّفْسَ عَنِ الْهَوَىٰ ﴿٤٠﴾ فَإِنَّ الْجَنَّةَ هِيَ الْمَأْوَىٰ ﴿٤١﴾ ﴿النازعات﴾

As for the one who feared standing before his Lord and restrained his soul from base desires (40) Truly Paradise will be his home (41)

Al-Nazi'āt (Those That Rise) 79:40-41

كَلَّا إِنَّ كِتَابَ الْأَبْرَارِ لَفِي عِلِّيِّينَ ﴿١٨﴾ وَمَا أَدْرَاكَ مَا عِلِّيُّونَ ﴿١٩﴾ كِتَابٌ

مَرْقُومٌ ﴿٢٠﴾ يَشْهَدُهُ الْمُقَرَّبُونَ ﴿٢١﴾ إِنَّ الْأَبْرَارَ لَفِي نَعِيمٍ ﴿٢٢﴾ عَلَى

الْأَرَائِكِ يَنْظُرُونَ ﴿٢٣﴾ تَعْرِفُ فِي وُجُوهِهِمْ نَضْرَةَ النَّعِيمِ ﴿٢٤﴾ يُسْقَوْنَ

مِنْ رَحِيقٍ مَخْتُومٍ ﴿٢٥﴾ خِتَامُهُ مِسْكٌ ۚ وَفِي ذَلِكَ فَلْيَتَنَافَسِ الْمُتَنَافِسُونَ

﴿٢٦﴾ وَمِزَاجُهُ مِنْ تَسْنِيمٍ ﴿٢٧﴾ عَيْنًا يَشْرَبُ بِهَا الْمُقَرَّبُونَ ﴿٢٨﴾

﴿المطففين﴾

Nay, truly the record of the pious is in *Illiyyin* (18) And what will convey
to thee what *Illyyun* is? (19) A record inscribed (20) Witnessed by those
brought near (to God) (21) Truly the pious shall be in bliss (22) Upon
couches, gazing (23) You shall recognize on their faces the radiance of
bliss (24) They are given a drink of pure wine, sealed (25) The seal of
which is fragranced with musk - and for that let those strive (26) And
mixed with water of Tasnīm (27) A spring from which those brought
near will drink (28)

Al-Mutaffifīn (Those Who Give Short Measure) 83:18-28

يَا أَيُّهَا الْإِنْسَانُ إِنَّكَ كَادِحٌ إِلَىٰ رَبِّكَ كَدْحًا فَمُلَاقِيهِ ﴿٦﴾ فَأَمَّا مَنْ أُوتِيَ كِتَابَهُ بِيَمِينِهِ ﴿٧﴾ فَسَوْفَ يُحَاسَبُ حِسَابًا يَسِيرًا ﴿٨﴾ وَيَنْقَلِبُ إِلَىٰ أَهْلِهِ مَسْرُورًا ﴿٩﴾ ﴿الإنشقاق﴾

O mankind! Truly thou art laboring towards thy Lord, painfully struggling, but then you shall meet Him (6) And whoever is given his record in his right hand (7) He will receive an easy reckoning (8) And will return to his people joyously (9)

Al-Inshiqāq (The Splitting) 84:6-9

إِنَّ الَّذِينَ آمَنُوا وَعَمِلُوا الصَّالِحَاتِ لَهُمْ جَنَّاتٌ تَجْرِي مِنْ تَحْتِهَا الْأَنْهَارُ ۚ ذَٰلِكَ الْفَوْزُ الْكَبِيرُ ﴿١١﴾ ﴿البروج﴾

Truly those who believe and perform righteous deeds theirs shall be Gardens beneath which rivers flow. That is the supreme triumph (11)

Al-Burūj (The Great Constellations) 85:11

إِنَّ بَطْشَ رَبِّكَ لَشَدِيدٌ ﴿١٢﴾ إِنَّهُ هُوَ يُبْدِئُ وَيُعِيدُ ﴿١٣﴾ وَهُوَ الْغَفُورُ الْوَدُودُ ﴿١٤﴾ ذُو الْعَرْشِ الْمَجِيدُ ﴿١٥﴾ فَعَّالٌ لِمَا يُرِيدُ ﴿١٦﴾ ﴿البروج﴾

Truly the punishment of thy Lord is severe (12) Truly it is He Who creates (life) and restores (life) (13) And He is the Forgiving, the Loving (14) Owner of the Throne of Glory (15) Doer of whatever He will (16)

Al-Burūj (The Great Constellations) 85:12-16

قَدْ أَفْلَحَ مَنْ تَزَكَّىٰ ﴿١٤﴾ وَذَكَرَ اسْمَ رَبِّهِ فَصَلَّىٰ ﴿١٥﴾ بَلْ تُؤْثِرُونَ الْحَيَاةَ الدُّنْيَا ﴿١٦﴾ وَالْآخِرَةُ خَيْرٌ وَأَبْقَىٰ ﴿١٧﴾ إِنَّ هَٰذَا لَفِي الصُّحُفِ الْأُولَىٰ ﴿١٨﴾ صُحُفِ إِبْرَاهِيمَ وَمُوسَىٰ ﴿١٩﴾ ﴿الأعلى﴾

Prosperous is he who purifies himself (14) Remembers the name of his Lord and prays (15) But, nay, you prefer the life of this world (16) Although the Hereafter is better and more enduring (17) Truly this is in the scriptures of old (18) The scriptures of Abraham and Moses (19)

Al-Alā (The Most Exalted) 87:14-19

وُجُوهٌ يَوْمَئِذٍ نَاعِمَةٌ ﴿٨﴾ لِسَعْيِهَا رَاضِيَةٌ ﴿٩﴾ فِي جَنَّةٍ عَالِيَةٍ ﴿١٠﴾ لَا

تَسْمَعُ فِيهَا لَاغِيَةً ﴿١١﴾ فِيهَا عَيْنٌ جَارِيَةٌ ﴿١٢﴾ فِيهَا سُرُرٌ مَرْفُوعَةٌ ﴿١٣﴾

وَأَكْوَابٌ مَوْضُوعَةٌ ﴿١٤﴾ وَنَمَارِقُ مَصْفُوفَةٌ ﴿١٥﴾ وَزَرَابِيُّ مَبْثُوثَةٌ ﴿١٦﴾

﴿الغاشية﴾

Some faces on that Day will be calm (8) Well-pleased with their endeavours (9) In a high Garden (10) Wherein they will hear no idle talk (11) Therein is a flowing spring (12) Therein are couches raised (13) And goblets placed (14) And cushions arrayed (15) And carpets spread out (16)

Al-Ghāshiyah (The Overwhelming Event) 88:8-16

كَلَّا إِذَا دُكَّتِ الْأَرْضُ دَكًّا ﴿٢١﴾ وَجَاءَ رَبُّكَ وَالْمَلَكُ صَفًّا ﴿٢٢﴾ وَجِيءَ

يَوْمَئِذٍ بِجَهَنَّمَ ۚ يَوْمَئِذٍ يَتَذَكَّرُ الْإِنْسَانُ وَأَنَّىٰ لَهُ الذِّكْرَىٰ ﴿٢٣﴾ يَقُولُ يَا لَيْتَنِي

قَدَّمْتُ لِحَيَاتِي ﴿٢٤﴾ فَيَوْمَئِذٍ لَا يُعَذِّبُ عَذَابَهُ أَحَدٌ ﴿٢٥﴾ وَلَا يُوثِقُ

وَثَاقَهُ أَحَدٌ ﴿٢٦﴾ يَا أَيَّتُهَا النَّفْسُ الْمُطْمَئِنَّةُ ﴿٢٧﴾ ارْجِعِي إِلَىٰ رَبِّكِ

رَاضِيَةً مَرْضِيَّةً ﴿٢٨﴾ فَادْخُلِي فِي عِبَادِي ﴿٢٩﴾ وَادْخُلِي جَنَّتِي ﴿٣٠﴾

﴿الفجر﴾

Nay, but when the earth is crushed (to dust), crushing upon crushing (21) And your Lord comes with the angels, rank upon rank (22) And on that Day, Hell is brought near (within sight), that Day man will remember; but how will that remembrance benefit him? (23) He will say, "If only I had provided (good deeds) beforehand for my (future) life!" (24) On that Day no one punishes as He will punish (25) And no one binds as He will bind (26) O thou soul at peace! (27) Return unto thy Lord, well-pleased, well-pleasing (28) Enter among My servants (29) And enter My Garden (30)

Al-Fajr (Dawn) 89:21-30

فَلَا اقْتَحَمَ الْعَقَبَةَ ﴿١١﴾ وَمَا أَدْرَاكَ مَا الْعَقَبَةُ ﴿١٢﴾ فَكُّ رَقَبَةٍ ﴿١٣﴾ أَوْ

إِطْعَامٌ فِي يَوْمٍ ذِي مَسْغَبَةٍ ﴿١٤﴾ يَتِيمًا ذَا مَقْرَبَةٍ ﴿١٥﴾ أَوْ مِسْكِينًا ذَا

مَتْرَبَةٍ ﴿١٦﴾ ثُمَّ كَانَ مِنَ الَّذِينَ آمَنُوا وَتَوَاصَوْا بِالصَّبْرِ وَتَوَاصَوْا بِالْمَرْحَمَةِ

﴿١٧﴾ أُولَٰئِكَ أَصْحَابُ الْمَيْمَنَةِ ﴿١٨﴾ ﴿البلد﴾

But he has not attempted the steep path (11) And what will explain to thee the steep path? (12) (It is) freeing a slave (13) Or giving food upon a day of extreme hunger (14) To an orphan near of kin (15) Or a needy (down) in the dust (16) Then he will be one of those who believe and urge one another to patience and urge one another to compassion (17) Those are the inhabitants of the right (18)

Al-Balad (The City) 90:11-18

وَلَسَوْفَ يُعْطِيكَ رَبُّكَ فَتَرْضَىٰ ﴿٥﴾ أَلَمْ يَجِدْكَ يَتِيمًا فَآوَىٰ ﴿٦﴾ وَوَجَدَكَ ضَالًّا فَهَدَىٰ ﴿٧﴾ وَوَجَدَكَ عَائِلًا فَأَغْنَىٰ ﴿٨﴾ فَأَمَّا الْيَتِيمَ فَلَا تَقْهَرْ ﴿٩﴾ وَأَمَّا السَّائِلَ فَلَا تَنْهَرْ ﴿١٠﴾ وَأَمَّا بِنِعْمَةِ رَبِّكَ فَحَدِّثْ ﴿١١﴾ ﴿الضحى﴾

And surely thy Lord shall give unto thee so that thou shalt be well-pleased (5) Did He not find thee an orphan and shelter thee? (6) Found thee wandering and guided thee? (7) Found thee destitute and enriched thee? (8) Therefore the orphan oppress not (9) And as for the beggar, repel not (10) And of the blessings of thy Lord proclaim! (11)

Al-Duhā (The Morning Brightness) 93:5-11

فَإِنَّ مَعَ الْعُسْرِ يُسْرًا ﴿٥﴾ إِنَّ مَعَ الْعُسْرِ يُسْرًا ﴿٦﴾ فَإِذَا فَرَغْتَ فَانْصَبْ ﴿٧﴾ وَإِلَىٰ رَبِّكَ فَارْغَبْ ﴿٨﴾ ﴿الشرح﴾

For truly with hardship comes ease! (5) Truly with hardship comes ease! (6) So when thou art free, apply thyself (in devotion) (7) And to thy Lord turn (all) thy attention (8)

Al-Sharh (The Opening of The Heart) 94:5-8

لَقَدْ خَلَقْنَا الْإِنْسَانَ فِي أَحْسَنِ تَقْوِيمٍ ﴿٤﴾ ثُمَّ رَدَدْنَاهُ أَسْفَلَ سَافِلِينَ ﴿٥﴾ إِلَّا الَّذِينَ آمَنُوا وَعَمِلُوا الصَّالِحَاتِ فَلَهُمْ أَجْرٌ غَيْرُ مَمْنُونٍ ﴿٦﴾ فَمَا يُكَذِّبُكَ بَعْدُ بِالدِّينِ ﴿٧﴾ أَلَيْسَ اللَّهُ بِأَحْكَمِ الْحَاكِمِينَ ﴿٨﴾ ﴿التين﴾

Truly We created man in the best stature (4) Then We reduced him to the lowest of the low (5) Save those who believe and perform righteous deeds; for theirs shall be a reward unceasing (6) So what then after this makes you deny the judgement? (7) Is God not the most just of judges? (8)

Al-Tīn (The Fig) 95:4-8

اقْرَأْ بِاسْمِ رَبِّكَ الَّذِي خَلَقَ ﴿١﴾ خَلَقَ الْإِنْسَانَ مِنْ عَلَقٍ ﴿٢﴾ اقْرَأْ
وَرَبُّكَ الْأَكْرَمُ ﴿٣﴾ الَّذِي عَلَّمَ بِالْقَلَمِ ﴿٤﴾ عَلَّمَ الْإِنْسَانَ مَا لَمْ يَعْلَمْ ﴿٥﴾
﴿العلق﴾

Read! In the name of thy Lord who created (1) Created man from a
blood clot (2) Read! Thy Lord is Most Bountiful (3) Who taught by the
Pen (4) Taught man what he knows not (5)

Al-Alaq (The Clot) 96:1-5

إِنَّ الَّذِينَ آمَنُوا وَعَمِلُوا الصَّالِحَاتِ أُولَٰئِكَ هُمْ خَيْرُ الْبَرِيَّةِ ﴿٧﴾ جَزَاؤُهُمْ عِنْدَ رَبِّهِمْ جَنَّاتُ عَدْنٍ تَجْرِي مِنْ تَحْتِهَا الْأَنْهَارُ خَالِدِينَ فِيهَا أَبَدًا ۖ رَضِيَ اللَّهُ عَنْهُمْ وَرَضُوا عَنْهُ ۚ ذَٰلِكَ لِمَنْ خَشِيَ رَبَّهُ ﴿٨﴾ ﴿البينة﴾

Truly those who believe and perform righteous deeds, they are the best of creation (7) Their reward with their Lord is Gardens of Eden, beneath which rivers flow abiding therein forever. God is well-pleased with them and they well-pleased with Him. This is for whoever stands in awe of his Lord (8)

Al-Bayyinah (The Clear Evidence) 98:7-8

إِنَّ الْإِنْسَانَ لَفِي خُسْرٍ ﴿٢﴾ إِلَّا الَّذِينَ آمَنُوا وَعَمِلُوا الصَّالِحَاتِ وَتَوَاصَوْا
بِالْحَقِّ وَتَوَاصَوْا بِالصَّبْرِ ﴿٣﴾ ﴿العصر﴾

Truly mankind is in a (state of) loss (2) Save those who believe, perform righteous deeds, urge one another to the truth and urge one another to patience (3)

Al-Asr (The Time) 103:2-3

فَسَبِّحْ بِحَمدِ رَبِّكَ وَاستَغفِرهُ ۚ إِنَّهُ كانَ تَوّابًا ﴿٣﴾ ﴿النصر﴾

Glorify the praise of your Lord and seek His forgiveness. Truly He is ever an acceptor or repentance (3)

Al-Nasr (The Help) 110:3

Bibliography

The Holy Qur'an

English Translations:

Abdel Haleem, Muhammad A. S. *The Qur'an: A New Translation.* Oxford University Press, 2010

Ali, Abdullah Yusuf. *The Meaning of The Holy Qur'an.* Amana Publications, 2006

Asad, Mohammad. *The Message of The Qur'an: Translated and Explained.* The Book Foundation, 2003

Eaton, Gai. *Remembering God: Reflections on Islam.* The Islamic Texts Society, 2000

Helwa, A. *Secrets of Divine Love: A Spiritual Journey into the Heart of Islam.* Naulit Publishing House, 2020

Kabir, Helminski. *The Book of Revelations: A Sourcebook of Selections from the Qur'an with Interpretations by Mohammad Asad, Yusuf Ali, and Others.* The Book Foundation, 2005

Muhammad, Ghazi Bin. *Love in the Holy Qur'an: Expanded 7th Edition.* The Islamic Texts Society, 2013

Nasr, Seyyed Hossein. *The Study Quran: A New Translation and Commentary.* HarperOne, an Imprint of HarperCollins Publishers, 2015

Pickthall, Muhammad Marmaduke. *The Meaning of the Glorious Koran: An Explanatory Translation.* Kazi Publications Inc, 1996